MW01070323

How to Rescue Your Loved One
from Mormonism

How to Rescue Your Loved One from Mormonism

David A. Reed
and
John R. Farkas

Baker Books

A Division of Baker Book House Co
Grand Rapids, Michigan 49516

© 1994 by David A. Reed and John R. Farkas

Published by Baker Books
a division of Baker Book House Company
P.O. Box 6287, Grand Rapids, MI 49516–6287

Printed in the United States of America

All rights reserved. No part of this publication may be reproduced, stored in a retrieval system, or transmitted in any form or by any means—electronic, mechanical, photocopy, recording, or any other—without the prior written permission of the publisher. The only exception is brief quotations in printed reviews.

Library of Congress Cataloging-in-Publication Data

Reed, David A.
    How to rescue your loved one from Mormonism / by David A. Reed and John R. Farkas.
        p.   cm.
    Includes bibliographical references and indexes.
    ISBN 0–8010–7771–0
    1. Church of Jesus Christ of Latter-Day Saints—Controversial literature. 2. Mormon Church—Controversial literature. I. Farkas, John R. II. Title.
BX8645.R38   1994   94-3942
289.3—dc20

Unless otherwise noted, Scripture quotations are from the King James Version of the Bible.

Scripture quotations identified NKJV are from The New King James Version. Copyright © 1979, 1980, 1982, Thomas Nelson, Inc., Publishers.

Scripture quotations identified NIV are from the HOLY BIBLE, NEW INTERNATIONAL VERSION®. NIV®. Copyright © 1973, 1978, 1984 by International Bible Society. Used by permission of Zondervan Publishing House. All rights reserved.

Scripture quotations identified NEB are from *The New English Bible.* © The Delegates of the Oxford University Press and The Syndics of The Cambridge University Press 1961, 1970. Reprinted by permission.

Scripture quotations identified NRSV are from the New Revised Standard Version of the Bible, copyright 1989 by the Division of Christian Education of the National Council of the Churches of Christ in the USA. Used by permission.

Contents

Acknowledgments

We would like to thank Phyllis Farkas for her insightful comments and corrections to the manuscript, and Penni Reed for her patient endurance.

Also, we have special thanks and gratitude to the writers and researchers who went before us for making their information available for our use.

But above all we thank our Lord and Savior Jesus Christ for giving us this opportunity to witness for the truth of his gospel.

Preface

This book is the product not only of academic research but also of personal experience. This experience comes not only from getting people out of Mormonism and similar controlling sects but also from personal involvement—indoctrination and membership—in them ourselves. We have stood in both places and have seen the problem from both sides of the issue.

John R. Farkas

It is an early morning late in February 1984. As usual I am reading the scriptures while eating breakfast.

I am in the Book of Mormon, 1 Nephi 18:25. This verse mentions the cow, ox, ass, horse, goat, and wild goat. This morning is a little unusual, though, in that I find myself questioning how some of these animals could have been in the New World.

Didn't historians say that full-size horses were not in the New World until the European explorers and settlers arrived? This thought had occurred to me at least once before, I think, while I was investigating the Church of Jesus Christ of Latter-day Saints, the Mormons, or LDS as it is usually called.

But this time the questions stayed with me and I found myself thinking about other questions that I apparently had suppressed in the past. I now had become teachable and open, a necessary prerequisite to the receiving of productive witnessing.

I didn't recognize it then, but for about the previous four to six months my testimony had shifted. It didn't, as it once had, include Joseph Smith and the Book of Mormon.

Starting with the late February period when I questioned the presence of certain animals in the New World, and continuing for about two months, I seldom had a complete night's sleep. Almost every night I woke up to study for one or two hours, in addition to using all of my free time for the same thing. By the end of February I had shared my doubts with my resident Mormon expert, my born-again Christian wife, Phyllis.

In 1975, when I had joined the LDS Church, she became a Christian and started her critical studies of Mormonism. I had gone on to become the elders quorum president of the Fairport Ward (1981–1984) and in early 1984 of the newly reorganized Rochester 1st Ward, both in the Rochester, New York, Stake, while Phyllis became an expert in Mormon studies and acquired a very extensive library. When I asked her for certain information, I almost always had it within minutes.

By March 15 I had made up my mind to leave the Mormon Church. I knew it when I woke up that night and removed my temple garments.[1] I felt free!

My drive to study and learn continued, this time to grow in depth and breadth in Mormon studies and about the Bible and Jesus Christ.

On March 20, 1984, I sent Stake President Dale Dallon my letter of resignation. The reasons I noted in my letter were the changes in the *Book of Commandments* versus Doctrine and Covenants, changes to the Book of Mormon, conflicts between early and present-day teachings, and the translation of the *Book of Abraham*. I stated that "Joseph Smith was a fraud and has pulled off one of the greatest hoaxes ever!!!" My name was formally taken off the Church rolls at a Church court on May 10.

---

1. Mormons who have been through the temple for their "endowments" are required to wear "temple garments" continually from that time forward. The original temple garment consisted of a one-piece white union suit reaching from the neck to the wrists and ankles. Shortened sleeves and legs are now approved. The garments have four symbolic markings: a square on the right breast and a compass on the left, a stitched line over the navel and over the right knee. Masons have said that these markings remind them of the square and the compass pressed against the body in those locations during Masonic rituals.

How did I get involved with the Mormon Church? It was my wife's fault. I say that now, partially in jest.

In 1974 when I became concerned with the food supply chain and saw a need to have a long-term supply of food at home, Phyllis said, "The Mormons do that sort of thing. I'll send them a letter in Salt Lake City." Well, she did, and the LDS missionaries brought the answer to us. We both took the missionary lessons. I joined in July 1975. Phyllis became a Christian.

During that time I asked a very significant question without realizing how significant it was. I said to Phyllis, "If we are both praying to the same God, why are we getting different answers?" Now I realize that the Mormon gods are not of the Bible. Mormonism is *not* Christian.

When I left the Mormon Church on March 15, 1984, I was left essentially with the beliefs that I had held in 1974 before I joined the Church. I was still a spiritual infant. I believed in a supreme being, a God, but I did not accept the Bible as the Word of God and I did not accept Jesus Christ as his Son and my Savior.

I had a desire to know, so I studied the Bible and books about the Bible, associated with Christians, attended Christian Sunday services and Sunday school. Through this I came to know that the Bible is the Word of God, and I came to know the real Lord Jesus Christ.

But even at this point I didn't know I was "saved."

Only after prayerful reading of John 3:16 with my friend Ross Amico—the then director of a group that was to become Berean Christian Ministries, an organization dedicated to exposing cults—did I fully realize the truth of John 3:16 and that I was the "whosoever" mentioned in this verse. The promise that I could claim was the important thing.

Ironically, I accepted Jesus in a Palmyra, New York, Christian church that is adjacent to the Mormon chapel where I had been baptized nine years earlier to the very week. On Sunday, July 19, 1984, I answered an altar call at a Webster, New York, Christian church and made public my faith in the real Lord Jesus Christ. Now I know of the simplicity and beauty of his gospel.

I also had a drive to share my newfound knowledge and faith with others, both Mormons and non-Mormons. It is interesting that I had never had anything like this drive to share Mormonism with others. I had not been a good member missionary. In fact, in my last four to six months of LDS Church membership my feelings against missionary work surfaced. This became evident to me as my bishop attempted to increase missionary activity in our ward, and I only gave him passive support; but I didn't understand it then.

The Mormon people are a great people. They and their Church have many characteristics that I found appealing. They are hardworking, conservative, successful, well organized, and they give great socials. They are good people in a worldly sense and should have the real Jesus Christ of the Bible.

Using the Bible, they present some convincing arguments that appear to support their doctrine. It is important for Christians to know the Bible and to know the real Lord Jesus Christ. A weak Christian is no match against the Mormon story; it is very appealing. It is easier to keep people from joining the Mormon Church than to get members out.

Groups like Berean Christian Ministries and publications like *Comments from the Friends* perform a multifunction service in combatting the false, non-Christian teachings of the Mormon Church and similar groups. They help to educate Christians, Mormons, and others; they organize activities that individuals could not handle; they provide support for those trying to get out from under the control of Mormonism and similar organizations.

My wife, Phyllis, is editor of *The Berean Report*. For over five years I have coordinated the Berean Christian Ministries outreach at the Mormon Hill Cumorah Pageant held annually in July near Palmyra, New York. It is the largest outdoor pageant in America, and up to 100,000 people attend each year. Over 13,000 pieces of Christian literature have been distributed each year.

I am a graduate of the University of Connecticut with a B.S. degree in mechanical engineering, and I am a licensed New York State professional engineer. From 1962 to 1991 I worked at Xerox Corporation as a project engineer and a project engineering manager. One of the reasons I tell you these things is to illustrate that worldly accomplishment and intellectual capability are different from spiritual capability. I have often been asked how a person could believe Mormon doctrine, and I can understand why the question is asked. But when the Mormon missionaries came to our house, I was a spiritual baby, and they only taught the milk of the Mormon "gospel." The meat comes later. As Hebrews 5:14 says, I was not of full age: "But strong meat belongeth to them that are of full age, even those who by reason of use have their senses exercised to discern both good and evil." I was not able to discern the real gospel of Jesus Christ from the "gospel" the Mormon missionaries had.

Through the prayers of concerned Christians, including my wife, who persevered through a rough situation, I became teachable and then "of full age." I hope and pray that the biblical Jesus Christ is your Lord and Savior as he is mine.

David A. Reed

My early religious training was in a big, white Unitarian church in rural New England south of Boston, where, at age fourteen, I concluded that religion was "the opium of the people." Later I went on to Harvard University and found that such atheism was perfectly acceptable there. By the time I was twenty-two, however, I came to realize that godless evolution offered me only a pointless existence in a meaningless universe, followed by a "dead" end. I began to think about God again.

At that time a Jehovah's Witness was assigned to work alongside me at my job, so I began asking him questions about his beliefs. His answers amazed me. It was the first time that I had ever heard religious thoughts presented in a tightly-knit, logical framework. In no time I became a very zealous Witness myself and remained in the Watchtower organization for thirteen years serving as a full-time minister and a congregation elder.

I married Penni Scaggs, who was raised in the organization and was also a zealous Witness. Between the two of us we conducted home Bible studies with dozens of people and brought well over twenty of them into the sect as baptized Jehovah's Witnesses. What interrupted this life of full dedication to the Watchtower Society? In one word, *Jesus*. Let me explain.

When Penni and I were at a large Witness convention, we saw a handful of opposers picketing outside. One of them carried a sign that said, "Read the Bible, not the *Watchtower.*" We had no sympathy for the picketers, but we did feel convicted by this sign, because we knew that we had been reading Watchtower publications to the exclusion of reading the Bible. Later on we actually counted up all of the materials that the organization expected JWs to read. The books, magazines, lessons, and other materials added up to over three thousand pages each year, compared with fewer than two hundred pages of Bible reading assigned, and most of that was in the Old Testament. The majority of Witnesses were so bogged down by the three thousand pages of the organization's literature that they seldom got around to the Bible reading.

After seeing the picket sign, Penni turned to me and said, "We should be reading the Bible *and* the Watchtower material." I agreed, so we began doing regular personal Bible reading with the aim of becoming better Jehovah's Witnesses.

As we read the New Testament we were impressed with Jesus as a person: what he said and did, and how he treated people. We wanted to be his followers. Especially we were struck with how Jesus responded to the hypocritical religious leaders of the day, the scribes and Pharisees. I remember reading over and over again the accounts of how the Pharisees objected to Jesus' healing on the Sabbath, his disciples' eating with unwashed hands, and other details of behavior that violated their traditions. How I loved Jesus' response: "You hypocrites, Isaiah aptly prophesied about you, when he said, 'This people honors me with their lips, yet their heart is far removed from me. It is in vain that they keep worshiping me, because they teach commands of men as doctrines'" (Matt. 15:7–9, the Watchtower's *New World Translation*).

"Commands of men as doctrines!" That thought stuck in my mind, and I began to realize that, in fulfilling my role as an elder, I was acting more like a Pharisee than a follower of Jesus. For example, the elders were the enforcers of all sorts of petty rules about dress and grooming, and this reminded me of the Pharisees who condemned Jesus' disciples for eating with unwashed hands.

Grooming was not the real issue, however. For me it was a question of whose disciple I was. Was I a follower of Jesus or an obedient servant to a human hierarchy? The elders who eventually put me on trial knew that that was the real issue, too. They kept asking, "Do you believe that the Watchtower Society is God's organization? Do you believe that the Society speaks as Jehovah's mouthpiece?"

With the new perspective that I was gaining from Bible reading, it upset me to see the organization elevate itself above Scripture, as it did when the December 1, 1981, *Watchtower* said: "Jehovah God has also provided his visible organization. . . . Unless we are in touch with this channel of communication that God is using, we will not progress along the road to life, no matter how much Bible reading we do" (p. 27). It really disturbed me to see those men elevate themselves above God's Word.

Since I was not allowed to speak out at the meetings, I decided to try writing. That's when I started publishing the newsletter *Comments from the Friends.* The elders wanted to put me on trial for publishing it, but my wife and I simply stopped going to the Kingdom Hall. By that time most of our former friends there had become quite hostile toward us. One young man called on the phone and threatened to "come over and take care of" me if he got another newsletter. And another Witness actually left a couple of death threats on our answering machine.

It was a great relief to be out from under the oppressive yoke of that organization. But we now had to face the challenge of where to go and what to believe. It takes some time to rethink your entire religious outlook on life. And we had not yet come into fellowship with Christians outside the JW organization.

All Penni and I knew was that we wanted to follow Jesus and that the Bible contained all the information we needed. We were amazed at what we found in prayerfully reading the New Testament over and over again—things that we had never appreciated before, such as the closeness that the early disciples enjoyed with the risen Lord, the activity of the Holy Spirit in the early church, and Jesus' words about being born again.

All those years we were Jehovah's Witnesses, the Watchtower had taken us on a guided tour through the Bible. We gained a lot of knowledge about the Old Testament, and we could quote a lot of Scriptures, but we never heard the gospel of salvation in Christ. We never learned to depend on Jesus for our salvation and to look to him personally as our Lord. Everything centered around the Watchtower's works program, and people were expected to come to Jehovah God through the organization.

When I realized from reading Romans 8 and John 3 that I needed to be born of the Spirit, I was afraid at first. Jehovah's Witnesses believe that born-again people who claim to have the Holy Spirit are actually possessed by demons. And so I feared that if I prayed out loud to turn my life over to Jesus Christ, some demon might be listening, and the demon might jump in and possess me, pretending to be the Holy Spirit. (Many Jehovah's Witnesses live in constant fear of the demons. Some of our friends would even throw out second-hand furniture and clothing, fearing that the demons could enter their homes through those articles.) But then I read Jesus' words in Luke 11:9–13. In a context where he was teaching about prayer and casting out unclean spirits, Jesus said: "So I say to you, ask, and it will be given to you; seek, and you will find; knock, and it will be opened to you. For everyone who asks receives, and he who seeks finds, and to him who knocks it will be opened. If a son asks for bread from any father among you, will he give him a stone? Or if he asks for a fish, will he give him a serpent instead of a fish? Or if he asks for an egg, will he offer him a scorpion? If you then, being evil, know how to give good gifts to your children, how much more will your heavenly Father give the Holy Spirit to those who ask Him!" (NKJV).

I knew after reading those words that I could safely ask for Christ's Spirit (Rom. 8:9) without fearing that I would receive a demon. So, in the early morning privacy of our kitchen I proceeded to confess my need for salvation and to commit my life to Christ.

Today Penni teaches fifth grade in a Christian school that has students from about seventeen different churches. She really enjoys it, because she can tie the Scriptures into all sorts of subjects. I publish *Comments from the Friends* as a quarterly aimed at reaching Jehovah's Witnesses with the gospel and helping Christians who are talking to JWs.

Although the thrust of my outreach ministry is toward Jehovah's Witnesses, I also take advantage of opportunities to share the gospel with Mormons and have had numerous conversations with them—on the street where they were canvassing for potential converts and in my home when I have accepted their offer of a free copy of the Book of Mormon, which they personally deliver as a way to start weekly discussions. My research on Mormonism started out as preparation for such visits by the missionaries.

The most important lesson Penni and I have learned since leaving the Jehovah's Witnesses is that Jesus is not just a historical figure that we read about. He is alive and is actively involved with Christians today, just as he was back in the first century, A.D. He personally saves us, teaches us, and leads us. This personal relationship with God through his Son Jesus Christ is wonderful! The individual who knows Jesus and follows him will not even think about following anyone else: "And a stranger will they not follow, but will flee from him; for they know not the voice of strangers. . . . My sheep hear my voice, and I know them, and they follow me: And I give unto them eternal life; and they shall never perish, neither shall any man pluck them out of my hand" (John 10:5, 27–28).

Looking back, I realize that I was truly blessed because I helped others escape from the Watchtower: my dear wife, her parents, my three brothers, and most of my in-laws—not to mention numerous others we have encountered since then in our public ministry. But in all these cases I am convinced that I merely assisted as an instrument while the rescue was actually accomplished by the Lord Jesus Christ, of whom it is said, "If the Son sets you free, you will be free indeed" (John 8:36 NIV).

What We Learned

The first book we co-authored, *Mormons Answered Verse by Verse* (Baker Book House, 1992), is designed to help Christians respond biblically to the misuse of Scripture by LDS missionaries. It is already being used widely, wherever such encounters take place. It upholds the gospel of Jesus Christ against "another gospel" that some claim to have received from "an angel from heaven" (Gal. 1:6–8).

Besides teaching us the value of true Christianity in contrast to counterfeits, our experiences with the cults have also given us considerable knowledge of the mechanics of mind control and the steps that are necessary to break its stranglehold and to deprogram its victims. We learned the hard way. It is our hope that this book will make matters easier for others.

Introduction

Those of us involved with Christian outreach to Mormons always receive a steady stream of mail from people who have a spouse, relative, or friend in the LDS Church. Invariably these letters express dismay at the loved one's involvement with the sect, coupled with a sense of frustration after unsuccessful attempts to persuade him or her to quit.

In the case of a married couple what sometimes happens is this. The husband initially hears that his wife is studying with two clean-cut young men (or women) who come to the house every Wednesday afternoon.

He may answer with a casual "That's nice, dear," or, he may say, "Fine, as long as I don't have to get involved." But the reaction is too often one of disinterested tolerance—that is, until he finds out that the men are Mormon missionaries and that his wife will soon be joining them in worship at their chapel on Sundays, going to a Relief Society[1] weekly meeting, receiving routine visits from men and women members eager for both of them to join the church, and holding a Monday night Family Home Evening.[2]

A husband's disinterest may then transform into opposition. He may have heard the Mormons called everything from cultists to polygamists, and he does not want his wife involved with such

---

1. A women's organization, reputedly the oldest in the United States.

2. Family Home Evening is an institutionalized Monday night activity where Mormon families in their homes spend one to two hours together in a lesson period and a fun period usually using a study manual published by the Mormon Church.

a sect. As the two missionaries coach the wife on how to answer his objections with arguments he is unable to refute, the husband becomes increasingly frustrated. He knows Mormonism is wrong but lacks the ammunition to prove it. He feels himself ready to explode as he watches his wife become more and more wrapped up with the LDS Church, impervious to his attempts to dissuade her.

At this point a crossroads is reached. Feeling defeated and not wanting to lose touch with his wife, the man may decide to accompany her to Mormon services and to sit in on "discussions" to be conducted by two full-time missionary elders. Or, at the other extreme, the husband may separate from his wife, initiate divorce proceedings, and attempt to take custody of the children. Many husbands take one of these two opposite courses. But in between are many others who simply attempt to ride out the storm. They stop talking about religion to avoid the inevitable arguments, and they try to maintain some semblance of family life in spite of their spouses' increasingly heavy schedule of meeting attendance, hours set aside for "visiting teaching,"[3] and time spent in her "calling."[4] The marriage stays together, but the wife's religion remains a source of irritation and tension.

Perhaps the most universal expression heard from men in every one of those situations is this: "I love my wife deeply, but somehow she seems to have become a different person. It's as if there is an invisible wall between us."

Although many times it is the wife who is found at home and is therefore contacted by "two clean-cut young men" calling from house to house, often it is the husband who is initially drawn into the Mormon Church, perhaps through a workmate or business associate. When this happens, the effect on marriage and home life is just as disastrous.

A similar sort of emotional estrangement occurs when the one joining the Mormons is a son or daughter, a parent, a brother or sister, or even a close friend. It seems that the new LDS member

3. Two women are teamed together to keep in monthly contact with an assigned number of women members.

4. A calling is an ongoing responsibility given to each member by a local leader (the stake president or ward bishop). It may involve serving as a Sunday school teacher, a greeter, a chorister, or the bishop's executive secretary, to name just a few.

loses interest in the former relationship. The good times together are gone as the convert becomes preoccupied with the church. Warm friendship is replaced by a sort of detached tolerance.

After spending years writing letters to people desperate to rescue their loved ones from Mormonism, all the while wishing that the letters could be longer and more detailed and that we could write each one a book instead of a mere letter, we have finally forced ourselves to take the time out from busy schedules to actually write such a book.

In responding to letters, of course, we have often made use of existing tools in the field of cult ministry and have sent those in need a volume on LDS beliefs, a collection of testimonies by former Mormons, a book on the sect's history, or a copy of our own book, *Mormons Answered Verse by Verse*. None of these in themselves could serve as a complete guide to rescuing a loved one from Mormonism. Although these books provide the raw material needed for such an effort, none of them combine this with a step-by-step strategy. And even books aimed at equipping Christians to answer Mormon missionaries at the door generally do not detail the best approach to take when the Mormon is a member of the household or a close friend or workmate.

With over eight million people involved in Mormonism worldwide, including close to 4.3 million here in the United States (as of January 1991), and new converts being made at the rate of one thousand per day, there is a growing need for assistance to their millions of non-Mormon family members, relatives, and friends. The methods outlined in these pages have proved successful in helping many to rescue loved ones from Mormonism. Of course, the choice ultimately lies within the free will of each human heart faced with the option of sorting out fiction from historical reality and non-Biblical teachings from true ones. On several occasions we have heard Mormons say that even if someone showed them proof that Mormonism was false or that Joseph Smith was a false prophet, they would still remain members because the Holy Spirit told them it was true. They evidently had another spirit speaking to them (1 John 4:1) or their own motives for ignoring the facts. A high Mormon Church official has taught, "Our individual, personal testimonies are based on the witness of the spirit, not on any combination or accumulation of historical facts."[5] So, there can be no guarantee that this book, used correctly, will produce the desired result. Many who embrace Mormonism have this attitude, and, in some form, most truly believe that they have found the way to God's approval. But evidence to the contrary will have an impact on some of them. We are confident that this book will prove helpful, in many cases, to people who want to present such evidence with the aim of rescuing a loved one from Mormonism.

In assembling the documents used in this book for critical analysis and evaluation to show the changes in doctrinal teachings and the unique non-Christian teachings of the Mormon Church, we have used sources that have a variety of published dates. Some of these are covered by copyright law and are identified as such to the best of our ability. Our lawyer has advised us that our quoting or reproducing these portions meets the "fair use" criteria under Section 107 of the Copyright Act of 1976. As such we have not unlawfully used this material. Anyone intending to recopy it for use in another format may wish to obtain their own counsel as to the legal consequences of doing so. Full-page copies from original Mormon documents may be obtainable through a public library either from its own collection or from an interlibrary loan network.

---

5. Elder Dallin Oaks, a member of the Council of the Twelve Apostles, speaking at a Brigham Young University symposium on Doctrine and Covenants, as quoted in *The Salt Lake Tribune*, August 18, 1985, p. 2B, and the Ogden *Standard-Examiner*, August 24, 1985, p. 12.

1

"Rescue" from a Religion?

We speak of *rescue* when someone is trapped in a burning building, adrift at sea, or held captive by kidnappers, but we usually do not speak of rescuing someone from a religion. So, although some who have a family member, relative, or friend in the Mormon Church will immediately understand why we use this term in this book's title, it should be explained for the benefit of others.

People trapped in a place that they cannot get out of by themselves may need rescue. The Mormon Church is such a place, not because the building Mormons meet in is unsafe or a fire trap but because members of the sect are not free to leave or terminate their membership, at least not honorably and with their families intact. Thousands each year are formally excommunicated for criticizing the hierarchy or professing "false doctrine," according to commentator Anson Shupe, who cites such dissent as the most frequent cause among some twenty thousand excommunications annually since the early 1980s.[1] Mormons who contemplate leaving the organization know that they risk losing their LDS spouse, their children, their parents, and any other relatives or close friends in the faith. A man who leaves the church faces the possibility that his Mormon wife will listen to encour-

1. *The Darker Side of Virtue: Corruption, Scandal and the Mormon Empire* (Buffalo: Prometheus Books, 1991), p. 11.

23

agement from others in the sect to divorce him, since women are taught that achieving their heavenly goal in the afterlife depends on their being married in the temple to a Mormon man. From the point of view of these individuals, a religious organization is, in effect, holding their relatives hostage. Rescue is definitely in order.

Real-life drama grips the nation when news media report an injured child trapped at the bottom of a well or miners cut off by a cave-in. Police and fire departments have rescue teams trained to scale walls, if necessary, to bring life-saving medical help to those in need. In the case of people held hostage by armed terrorists or trapped by fire or fallen rock, rescue attempts are often risky. The very effort to reach them might easily trigger further harm with perhaps fatal consequences. In the case of Mormons a similar risk is involved. The would-be rescuer, hitherto viewed simply as an outsider to the sect, could suddenly be seen as an anti-Mormon who must be avoided; the relationship with that person that had been deteriorating because of the sect's influence might now be severed. So, the rescue attempt is something that is not to be viewed lightly nor to be undertaken carelessly or without regard to the inherent risks. Preparation should be made carefully and prayerfully before assaulting the fortress of Mormonism.

This involves breaking a popular taboo, the notion that it is not proper to talk about religion and especially not to "knock" someone else's religion. Is that notion valid? Must Christians respect Mormonism and refrain from attacking it? Of course, it is proper to respect anyone's sincerely held religious beliefs. But both Mormonism and biblical Christianity *encourage* talking about religion. Both send out missionaries for that purpose, and both train such individuals to be respectful when in dialogue with persons of other faiths.

When it comes to the question of attacking another religion, however, it is an established fact that Mormonism fired the first shot. The very beginning and foundation of the LDS Church is the alleged First Vision of the teenage Joseph Smith with the message that the other churches (sects) are "all wrong," their creeds "an abomination," and the professors of those creeds "corrupt" in God's sight (*Joseph Smith—History* 1:18–19, a Mormon scripture).[2]

Smith named names, too, including the Presbyterians, the Baptists, and the Methodists (1:5, 8, 9, 20). So, if others respond by saying that Mormonism is wrong, perhaps even an abomination, Mormons are free to produce evidence in support of their beliefs, but they have no right to cry "persecution!" or to say that they are being singled out for unprovoked attack. After all, we Christians certainly have a right to defend ourselves, seeing we do not believe that God said such things to Joseph Smith. In addition, we have the challenge of two top Mormon leaders who invite critical examination:

> If Joseph Smith was a deceiver, who wilfully attempted to mislead the people, then he should be exposed; his claims should be refuted, and his doctrines shown to be false, for the doctrines of an impostor cannot be made to harmonize in all particulars with divine truth.
> *Doctrines of Salvation*, Apostle Joseph Fielding Smith, vol. 1, 1954, p. 188.

> Take up the Bible, compare the religion of the Latter-day Saints with it, and see if it will stand the test.
> President Brigham Young, *Journal of Discourses*, vol. 16, May 1873, p. 46.

Christians should make a distinction, of course, between Mormonism and Mormons. Although the LDS Church can be shown to be wrong, its members in general do not thereby become enemies. Rather, they are victims. Jesus Christ, when chastising a Jewish nation that had strayed from the path laid out for it, reserved the strongest words for its religious leaders, whom he denounced as "hypocrites," "serpents," and "vipers" (Matt.

---

2. Also 1 Nephi 14:10, 17 in the Book of Mormon, another Mormon scripture, declares that there are " . . . two churches only; the one is the church of the Lamb of God, and the other is the church of the devil; wherefore, whoso belongeth not to the church of the Lamb of God belongeth to that great church, which is the mother of abominations; and she is the whore of all the earth. . . . the church of all the earth, whose founder is the devil." Moreover, Doctrine and Covenants 1:30, another Mormon scripture, speaks of the Mormon Church as coming "out of darkness, the only true and living church upon the face of the whole earth," and 20:1, 2 calls Joseph Smith, Jr., "the first elder" of "the Church of Christ in these last days."

23:29–33), but to the masses who were misled he gave the invitation, "Come unto me, all ye that labour and are heavy laden, and I will give you rest. Take my yoke upon you, and learn of me; for I am meek and lowly in heart: and ye shall find rest unto your souls" (11:28–29). Likewise, we today have a responsibility to expose the works of darkness (Acts 17:1–2, 10–11, 17; Eph. 5:11; 2 Tim. 4:2–4; Heb. 5:14; Jude 3); but when it comes to individuals caught up in that darkness our aim should be not to condemn them but rather to help them, just as "God sent not his Son into the world to condemn the world; but that the world through him might be saved" (John 3:17). So, although the material in this book could be used as ammunition for winning arguments, it is actually being presented for use in winning souls to Christ.

The strategy and techniques outlined in later chapters are specially tailored for prolonged discussions with a relative, a neighbor, a personal friend, or a workmate—someone seen on a regular basis over a period of time and someone whose continued friendship is valuable to you. A stranger appearing on your doorstep who is given the Bible with both barrels, so to speak, may come to Christ or may flee from your presence, never to return. That approach is too harsh and unnecessarily abrupt for someone you see on a regular basis, besides being too risky to use with your spouse or brother or next-door neighbor. With that in mind the approach outlined here is geared toward preserving the relationship while presenting the message. To that end it gets its points across slowly, gently, lovingly, and without open confrontation. The need for prompt action will be discussed in chapter 2 of this book. But, if you have been fighting over Mormonism before obtaining this book, you may need to allow a cooling-off period before switching gears to use this approach. It requires a considerable investment of time and patience, which is not too much to ask when a loved one's life is at stake. But it should also be noted that this approach is not limited to loved ones. It can be employed just as effectively in reaching out to a stranger. In that case, like the good Samaritan who invested in prolonged care for a wounded stranger, you, too, would make yourself a neighbor to him and adopt him as your loved one.

2

Don't Delay—Act Today!

As the old adage says, "An ounce of prevention is worth a pound of cure." It is usually much easier to keep people out of the Mormon Church than it is to get them out, and it is easier to free an individual from Mormonism if his or her involvement can be nipped in the bud. Timing is critical, and urgent action is in order if lessons are about to start or are under way. Generally speaking, the longer a person has been involved in Mormonism, the harder it is for that one to become teachable, that is, able to recognize non-Christian teaching and managed, whitewashed history.

As each new LDS doctrine is "proved" by Mormon instructors to their student and he accepts it as a valid belief, another step is added to the process of indoctrination. The effects of these lessons will eventually have to be undone, but the odds that this can be accomplished become slimmer as each new doctrine is accepted. Once the student prays "to know that the Book of Mormon is true" in response to the missionaries' invitation at the end of the first lesson, and the student has been led to interpret some emotional or physical feeling as an affirmative answer from God, it will be more difficult to discredit the teachings of the Mormon Church. Once the "investigator"[1] has accepted the second lesson's invitation to repent and be baptized, an attack on the Mormons may seem to him to be an attack on his personal decision

1. See glossary in appendix 3.

to leave sin behind and turn to God. And once the third lesson
has established the Mormon Church as God's restoration of true
Christianity, with a living prophet, twelve apostles, and priesthood authority, it will take time and effort to reestablish the fact
that there exist genuine Christians outside the Church of Jesus
Christ of Latter-day Saints. Once the six introductory lessons have
been completed and a date and time has been set for baptism and
for receiving new-members' lessons, extricating the new convert
grows into a major project that, even with intense effort, may not
bear fruit.

So, the main point to remember when a loved one starts getting involved with Mormonism is to avoid delay. As in fighting
an infectious disease that attacks the body, time is of the essence.

The need for speed is heightened by the speed with which Mormon missionaries present their case and draw new converts into
the sect. If the objections you raise at the outset are not factual
or are only partly correct or poorly presented and therefore are
overcome by the missionaries, you may have struck out. Unless
some powerful evidence against the sect is quickly brought into
play at this time, the game is over, at least for now.

Perhaps the mistake most commonly made in an attempt to
rescue a potential convert is failure to act soon enough. If you can
jump in at the very beginning, the best advice would be to do
something—to do almost anything—that will stop the lessons in
a kind, loving manner. Even a stalling tactic will help, if it will
allow you time to study the evidence against Mormonism and
better prepare your defense. Persuade your friend or loved one to
postpone the discussions until next week so that you can take
him or her out to eat at the appointed time this week, or schedule something else that will interfere with the discussions "just
this one time," and in the meantime prepare your case against
Mormonism.

On the other hand, if the discussions have already been in
progress for some time, you will have to proceed with extra caution. You should avoid doing anything that would make you look
like the "bad guy" and would vindicate the Mormons. At this
point a harsh ultimatum that your loved one must break off with
them could have disastrous results. And a series of unsupported,
nonfactual accusations (such as the often quoted but misinformed

charges that they are polygamists) will do a lot more harm than good. If the Mormons can disprove the initial charges you bring against them, you will lose your credibility, and they may be able to persuade their student not to listen to any future accusations. It is very important to have all your arguments correct and fully documented the first time around; otherwise, there may not be a second chance.

In any case, you should definitely avoid attempting to disprove Mormonism with the missionary "elders" present. This will only turn into a free-for-all debate, with the young "elders" coming up with an answer, excuse, or denial for everything you say. What they say may not necessarily be correct, but it will *appear* logical and correct. Unless you are thoroughly versed on the LDS Church and trained as a debater, the well-trained missionaries will shoot you down on every point. They will be the winners, and the new convert will be further cemented into the sect. Even Christians who are well versed in doctrine can have difficulty in refuting the Mormon missionaries with the Bible. One Lutheran seminarian said after meeting with two of them, "They had me for lunch." However, as we will show in forthcoming chapters, the Mormons' own scriptures and teaching manuals are their worst enemies when you can properly use them to expose LDS error.

So, it is important to plan your strategy, collect convincing evidence, and present it in the proper manner at an appropriate time and place. The remaining chapters of this book will help you do just that.

3

Overall Strategy

Failure to have an effective strategy can result in an encounter between a Christian and a Mormon that goes like this. The Christian shows the Mormon a Bible verse that contradicts LDS teaching. The Mormon then responds with another verse that he feels supports his beliefs. The Christian then counters with another verse, to which the Mormon replies with still another, and so forth. Such a Scripture-bashing discussion can be described as "biblical Ping-Pong." Doctrines and supporting verses bounce back and forth, perhaps for hours on end, with no tangible results other than the sweaty exhaustion that follows a real Ping-Pong game. Even if the Christian seems to have come off the winner in the debate, this carries no more weight with the Mormon than if it had been a mere Ping-Pong game he had lost. He is still not about to change his religion.

What is wrong with the above approach? Principally, timing. It is the timing that is wrong, not the biblical discussion itself. In fact, we wrote our book *Mormons Answered Verse by Verse* to aid in just such a discussion. Starting off with the Bible often works well when dealing with someone who has just become involved with the sect or with an "infant" Mormon who is not fully indoctrinated. But when dealing with a more mature member an effective strategy usually requires that consideration of Bible verses and doctrines come as a *second* step to be taken after the authority of the LDS Church has first been undermined through the use of materials and techniques that we will outline here and in the chapters to follow.

Why does a Christian who starts off with a doctrinal discussion supported by a barrage of Bible verses usually fail to make a dent in a seasoned Mormon's thinking? The reason is that this form of attack is based on a wrong assumption. It assumes that the Mormon believes certain things based on what he has read in the Bible and that he will change his beliefs if he is shown other verses as proof texts for a different doctrinal stance. But anyone making this assumption has already fallen victim to the sect's propaganda: the idea that Mormons are Bible readers who rely on it as authority. Actually, their Bible reading is diluted by also having to read and study their three additional sacred volumes: the Book of Mormon, Doctrine and Covenants, and Pearl of Great Price, one book each year in a four-year cycle. And they base their beliefs not on what they find in the Bible or even in the Book of Mormon but rather on what they are taught in lesson and training books, official speeches, Church newspaper and magazine articles, and books by top leaders.

This explains why a barrage of Scripture verses can bounce off a Mormon like so many Ping-Pong balls with no effect. He may look at the verses, but what he sees in his mind's eye is the LDS Church's interpretation of those verses. It is as if he is looking at the pages of the Bible through Mormon-colored glasses. So, the first step in your strategy must be to remove those distorted lenses. To accomplish this, you will have to get the Mormon to look at the LDS Church itself. You will need to demonstrate that its leaders have made repeated false prophecies, have changed doctrines and scriptures[1] back and forth, and have misled followers to their spiritual harm. In other words, they are not reliable guides to follow. The Mormon may then be forced to think for himself or herself; in effect, the Mormon-colored glasses may be removed. After this has been accomplished, it now becomes possible to enter into an effective verse-by-verse doctrinal discussion.

Although this strategy of undermining LDS Church authority as the first step and then examining Bible doctrine as the second step generally achieves the best results with fully indoctrinated

---

1. The changes to scripture we have in mind are not just the addition of new scripture but also include major changes to existing scripture.

Mormons, Christians untrained in countercult work almost always want to jump into the Bible right away. You may feel that way yourself. This is understandable because you are, no doubt, more familiar with the Bible than with Mormon history. At this point you would feel more comfortable with a biblical approach. You know some of the doctrinal differences between Christians and Mormons, and your natural response is to answer them on each point. But as long as you debate doctrines with your Mormon loved one, he or she will never see the forest for the trees, as the expression goes. At some point you must interrupt the issue-by-issue argument to focus attention on the big issue, the LDS Church itself.

Picture the Mormon Church, for a moment, as an ancient walled fort with archers and spearmen standing guard atop the wall. Your army surrounds the fort. Your archers shoot arrows at their counterparts on the wall, and your spearmen hurl missiles. Sometimes your men score a hit, and sometimes theirs do; but the battle goes nowhere. Nowhere, that is, until a contingent of your men stop trading shots with the enemy and instead, with helmets on their heads, shields on their backs, and shovels in their hands, dig around the base of the wall until it is undermined and collapses. As it falls, so do the host of archers and spearmen who stood atop it and were seemingly invulnerable only moments before.

Disputing with a well-versed Mormon over questions of deity, theology, and the afterlife can be like the archers and spearmen exchanging shots with those on the wall. But attacking the LDS Church itself, destroying its credibility by exposing its long history of error—this is akin to undermining the wall and causing it to topple over. When LDS Church authority falls, so do all the teachings and doctrines that depend on it for support.

It will take discipline on your part to ignore some of the "spears" and "arrows" thrown at you in the form of doctrinal challenges and to focus your attention and the attention of the Mormon on the LDS Church itself; but it will be well worth the effort. Once the leadership's authority is undermined, the doctrines will be much easier to deal with.

However, if you start off openly attacking the Mormon Church or obviously attempting to convert your friend, your attack may backfire and damage or destroy your relationship. Techniques to avoid such a disastrous result are discussed in the next chapter.

There is no set formula for witnessing to Mormons. Each witnessing opportunity is unique and different, and you must depend on the Holy Spirit to guide you and direct you. But there are some basic principles you can apply, things you should or should not do, and knowledge you should have or should gain. It will not be easy, and indeed it may be very frustrating, but you should do it anyway.

The ultimate goal is to lead the Mormon into a personal relationship with the one *true* God of the Bible. Keep in mind, he thinks he already worships the one true God. It is up to you to show him that he has a different God, a different Jesus, another gospel, and that he is breaking the first commandment. The strategy is to first undermine the Mormon's testimony and confidence in the Mormon Church organization—its teachings, official history, unique scriptures (Book of Mormon, Doctrine and Covenants, and Pearl of Great Price), and biblical misinterpretations. (Our previous book *Mormons Answered Verse by Verse* deals with biblical misinterpretations.) Your skills in selecting and presenting the information is important. The Mormon must become teachable. Until he is, it is usually best, as emphasized at the start of this chapter, to stay away from biblical proofs; such discussions usually turn into unprofitable Scripture bashing.

In any case, depend on the Holy Spirit to guide you. Before you witness you should know the following basics:

1. What does the Bible say about witnessing?
   "Warn the wicked . . . to save his life" (Ezek. 3:18–19). "Go ye therefore, and teach" (Matt. 28:19–20). "Preach the word" (2 Tim. 4:2–4). "In meekness instructing those that oppose" (2 Tim. 2:24–26). "But strong meat belongeth to them that are of full age" (Heb. 5:14). "Be ready always to give an answer" (1 Peter 3:15). "Earnestly contend for the faith" (Jude 3).

2. What do you need to witness to a Mormon?
   First, have a desire born of God. "Not by might, nor by power, but by my spirit, saith the LORD of hosts" (Zech. 4:6). Prayer is a powerful tool when witnessing. Use it regularly.

Second, be a strong Christian yourself. Have a personal relationship with God and be familiar with the biblical foundation of your own beliefs.

Third, know the role of "feelings" (the Mormon's personal testimony) and how "feelings" can be used as a substitute for factual proof, knowledge, and wisdom.

Fourth, know the subject. There is no substitute for detailed factual knowledge about Mormonism, its beliefs, and its church history.

Fifth, base your arguments on well-established factual information backed up by hard-copy documentation organized for quick and easy access. Actual photocopies from Mormon sources are much more powerful than paraphrased quotations from memory. Stay on the main subjects, such as those discussed later in this book.

Sixth, stay on one topic until you have presented all of your points. The Mormon will try to change the subject. Tell him gently that you will talk about *that* later, but now you are talking about *this*.

Before considering specific points to raise against the LDS Church, however, you would be wise to learn some techniques that work and to familiarize yourself with the tools you will need to use.

4

Techniques That Work

The best techniques to use in speaking with mature Mormons—those who are well past the missionary and new-members' lessons—depend on what you want to accomplish, how much time you have, and what you are able to invest. For example, suppose a young missionary at your door tells you that this is his last week in your community and that he will be flying back to Utah on Friday. In this case you should present a barrage of information that will quickly demolish Mormonism, conclude with your testimony and what it means to have Jesus in your life, and stuff a tract into his pocket as he leaves. Perhaps you will have planted or watered a seed that the Holy Spirit will use other Christians to cultivate later. That powerful presentation would be inappropriate, however, for a Mormon employee at your place of work assigned to work alongside you on a two-year project, or for a close friend or relative who has become involved with the sect. The rapid-fire approach you used with the missionary might give your workmate or relative something to think about, but the workmate would probably ask the boss for a transfer, and the relative might henceforth avoid you.

In the case of a fellow employee, relative, neighbor, or close friend you see on a regular basis an entirely different approach is called for. First, build rapport and credibility. Let your Christian manners and your lifestyle speak for you. Talk modestly about your relationship with the Lord and show a mild, friendly interest in your Mormon associate's religion. Ask questions (examples follow) that reflect curiosity rather than hostility or condemnation. To some extent a Mormon will feel obligated to assume the role of official spokesman when representing the Church to any outsider, but the more informal and relaxed you can make the circumstances, the more likely you will be able to truly communicate rather than simply exchange clichés.

If you start off openly attacking the Mormon Church or obviously attempting to convert your friend, you will likely trigger a defensive reaction. The stronger your attack or the more vigorous your conversion attempt, the greater will be the response that you will provoke. If you come to be viewed as a real enemy of the Church, that may mean an end to communication with this individual, or at least an end to communication on religious subjects.

Consider the example of Jesus Christ who, when he came to earth, did not loudly proclaim who he was but rather let his works speak for him. After fellowshiping with him for some time, his disciples still asked, "What manner of man is this, that even the wind and the sea obey him?" And it took the doubting Thomas the entire length of time he was associated with Jesus, and more, before he could finally confess Christ as "My Lord and my God" (John 20:28). Likewise, we are more effective if we let the facts speak for themselves in our conversations with Mormons than if we try to push them prematurely to the conclusion that they should reject the LDS Church and embrace a personal relationship with Jesus Christ.

The best example we can turn to for techniques is that of our Lord Jesus Christ, the master teacher. Besides miracles, he used well-chosen words to draw people to himself. And he had to teach some startling new concepts to those Jews who became his disciples. So we can learn much from his teaching methods that will help in our efforts to share the true gospel with Mormons.

Jesus knew how much his listeners would be able to absorb at one time; therefore, he did not try to overfeed them. Even after he had spent many months with the apostles, he told them, "I have yet many things to say unto you, but ye cannot bear them now" (John 16:12). The gospel consists of both "milk" and "solid food" (Heb. 5:12–14 NKJV). If you give solid food too soon to a baby, he will choke on it and spit it out. Realizing that it may take a long time for a mature Mormon to unlearn false LDS doctrines and relearn Bible truth, we should not give him too much to digest at one time.

Jesus could leave much of what he had to say until later, because he knew that the Holy Spirit would continue to teach the disciples—that "when He, the Spirit of truth, has come, He will guide you into all truth" (John 16:13 NKJV). We, too, should trust that the Holy Spirit will teach new believers today, just as he did in the first century A.D. We need not take it upon ourselves to correct every notion that a Mormon has in his head. The Holy Spirit will take over where we leave off.

Moreover, Jesus was a shepherd, not a cowboy. He did not ride herd on the sheep shooting guns and cracking whips like cowboys do in a cattle drive. No. He gently led the flock. Jesus called, and his sheep heard his voice and followed him. We can do the same by kindly presenting the gospel from the Word of God, confident that the sheep will hear and follow without our having to bully them into it.

Notice, too, Jesus' effective use of questions. Glancing quickly over any one of the four Gospel accounts, you will observe that many of his sentences had question marks at the end. Question marks are shaped like hooks (?) and they function much the same way in hooking onto answers and pulling them out through the other person's mouth. Jesus was highly skilled at using these "hooks." Rather than shower his listeners with information, he used questions to draw answers out of them, thereby causing them to think about the subject. A person can close his ears to facts he doesn't want to hear, but if a pointed question causes him to form the answer in his own mind, he can't escape the conclusion because it's a conclusion he has reached himself.

Generally speaking, you should ask only questions that you already know the answers to and can document. This is important because (1) the Mormon may not really know the correct answer, or (2) the Mormon may purposely evade the correct answer. But, when you know the answer yourself you can ask supplementary questions to teach him the facts or to draw out knowledge that he is concealing. For example, if you ask whether a

Prophet of the LDS Church ever taught that Adam of the Garden of Eden was God the Father (Elohim), and the Mormon either denies it or claims not to know, you can then go on to ask more specifically about Brigham Young, inquiring about references to this teaching in his writings. (See the discussion in chapter 13, "Strange Teachings.")

It takes patience to draw answers from the Mormon rather than provide them yourself. But, if you provide the answers, the effect can be quite different. For example, you can tell a Mormon: "You have been deceived. Joseph Smith is a false prophet and the LDS Church is a cult![1] You need to get saved!" But, if he has not yet reached those conclusions in his own mind, he is likely to become offended and to reject whatever else you have to say. So, if you want him to reach those conclusions, you must lead his thinking in that direction.

Rather than comment, "Look at what Isaiah says in chapter 44, verses 6 and 8! He says that no other gods exist, besides the LORD," you would do better to ask the Mormon to read the verses aloud and then ask, "Whom, do you think, the writer was referring to in this verse? What did he say about him?" The Mormon may not say the right answer out loud, but you will see his facial expression change when he gets the point.

Although a loved one who is beginning to look into the LDS Church should be warned boldly that it is a pseudo-Christian cult—*and should be supplied proof* of this to offset the Church's effective public relations campaign—that approach may be too strong for someone who has been involved for some time as an active member. In his or her case it may prove more effective to take a more roundabout, indirect approach. We have a scriptural example of this technique being used by the apostle Paul. He did not get up before his Greek audience in Athens and proclaim, "Your religion is false; I'm here to convert you to Christianity." Rather, he established common ground first by presenting it this way: " . . . as I passed by, and beheld your devotions, I found an altar with this inscription, TO THE UNKNOWN GOD. Whom

---

1. Today, in fact, even the average man on the street would discount and find such statements incredible because of the extensive public relations and publicity by the LDS Church.

therefore ye ignorantly worship, him declare I unto you" (Acts 17:23).

We ought to be aware, too, that Mormons may actually attempt to deny or cover up some of their more bizzare teachings and justify this by their concern for people like us who are "not ready" to encounter these concepts yet. For example, when one Christian householder asked a missionary whether he believed in only one God, the young Mormon answered enthusiastically in the affirmative. Yes! He believed in just one God.

"You don't believe in many gods?" the Christian asked again.

"No! Just one God, the same as you believe," came the reply.

But this householder was an *informed* Christian and knew to press the issue further by asking, "Do you mean to say that you believe there is only one God in all the entire universe?"

Now the Mormon began fidgeting. Looking down at his feet he admitted, "Well, no. We believe there is just one God for this planet. Naturally, other planets have their own gods. I thought we were just talking about this planet."[2]

This demonstrates that Mormons sometimes talk with their fingers crossed, so to speak. Not intending to harm you but rather to bless you through conversion to the LDS Church, they may hold back certain information while at the same time they supply other information that is actually misleading. This may take the form of using familiar words with different meanings, as in the case of the young missionary who claimed to "believe in only one God." He did not see himself as lying but rather as going out of his way to help the Christian by avoiding offensive language or concepts.

Similarly, Mormons typically object to Christian efforts to expose Mormonism by saying, "We don't attack you; why are you attacking us? Why not say only good things about each other?" But in doing this the Mormons conceal the fact that Mormonism's very reason for being rests on Joseph Smith's alleged First Vision with its message that the churches are "all wrong"

---

2. This missionary's response, although typical, reflects his own homegrown hybrid theology, mixing official LDS teaching with popular misconceptions thereof commonly repeated by less-knowledgeable Mormons. For information on what the LDS Church actually teaches in this regard, see chapter 8, "Gods and Goddesses," as well as our book *Mormons Answered Verse by Verse.*

and their members "corrupt."[3] So, it is the Mormons who attacked first. Christians are defending, not attacking. The Mormon argument that Christians should not attack Mormonism is merely a smoke screen.

The following list of dos and don'ts should prove helpful as a quick-reference guide to review before you enter discussions with Mormons:

Do love them. Let the love of Christ radiate from you.

Do "turn the other cheek" when you are abused verbally or even physically.

Do pray with Mormons before and after a discussion, but *you* lead the prayer and use it to teach Christian principles.

Do your homework. Know your Bible and the subject you are covering.

Do use only the King James Version of the Bible. It is the only one most Mormons recognize as valid.

Do discern the meaning of Mormon terminology. They use Christian terms, but with very different meanings. See the glossary in appendix 3.

Do become familiar with the LDS Church's canonized scriptures or *standard works*. Notice which Mormon doctrines are found in the *standard works*. This will enable you to deal with the typical Mormon defense that an embarrassing teaching "is not in the *standard works* and therefore is not really Mormon doctrine but just someone's opinion."

---

3. "My object in going to inquire of the Lord was to know which of all the sects was right, that I might know which to join. No sooner, therefore, did I get possession of myself, so as to be able to speak, than I asked the Personages who stood above me in the light, which of all the sects was right (for at this time it had never entered into my heart that all were wrong)—and which I should join. I was answered that I must join none of them, for they were all wrong; and the Personage who addressed me said that all their creeds were an abomination in his sight; that those professors were all corrupt; that: 'they draw near to me with their lips, but their hearts are far from me, they teach for doctrines the commandments of men, having a form of godliness, but they deny the power thereof'" (*Joseph Smith—History* 1:18–19).

"And he said unto me: Behold there are save two churches only; the one is the church of the Lamb of God, and the other is the church of the devil; wherefore, whoso belongeth not to the church of the Lamb of God belongeth to that great church, which is the mother of abominations; and she is the whore of all the earth" (1 Nephi 14:10).

Do learn to distinguish between valid and invalid references. Not all Mormon writers and writings are of equal authority. High status is given to statements by Prophets and Apostles speaking at official LDS Church functions, especially conferences, or published in Church manuals. The words of the living Prophet take precedence over those of his predecessors.

Do take control and keep control of discussions. Well-trained Mormons (such as missionaries) will try to change the subject rather than face embarrassing facts. Keep bringing them back to the subject at hand by saying, "We were talking about . . ." or "You didn't answer my question about . . ." Be polite but bold.

Do use questions as a teaching technique. Generally, only ask questions to which you know the answers. Ask questions that lead your listeners to question their own beliefs.

Do be prepared to document information that the Mormon has never heard or understood before.

Do require the Mormon to provide documentation and references for points he or she wishes to make.

Do stop to look up references you are given to be sure they are being used properly and in context.

Do maintain a low-keyed, soft, friendly approach in order to keep the door open for further discussions. Reserve a bolder and more aggressive approach for one-time meetings with strangers who are unlikely to return.

Do focus on important matters. Avoid wasting time on trivia.

Do arrange for a captive audience by inviting Mormons to your home for a meal and asking them to arrive an hour or two before dinnertime so you can talk together. This will make it more difficult for them to escape when their position becomes indefensible by "remembering" an urgent appointment or inventing another excuse to leave. They are already committed to remain for the meal.

Don't try to witness to Mormons if you are a new Christian yourself; especially do not try to witness to LDS missionaries. Remember, they are thoroughly trained to win you over.

Don't be rude or ridicule their beliefs. Always be polite.

Don't assume that the individuals you deal with know Mormon doctrine. Many members have little knowledge and understanding of their Church's unique teachings. Others comprehend everything. Some are aware of the strange doctrines but conceal this knowledge in an attempt to appear Christian.

Don't argue or get angry. If a discussion becomes irrational or heated, walk away.

Don't try to cover too many subjects in one sitting. It is better to cover one subject thoroughly than to touch on several matters and not bring any to a conclusion.

Don't let the Mormon get away with speaking in generalities. Any accusation such as "The Bible is all wrong," or, "You people deal in half-truths and misrepresentations," should be challenged for lack of specific examples.

Don't place stumbling blocks before Mormons, such as offering them coffee, tea, or alcoholic beverages, or smoking in their presence.

Don't agree to pray about the truth of the Book of Mormon. Since God has already said not to accept "another gospel" (Gal. 1:6–9), this would be praying to discern whether you should do something God has already said not to do. It would be sidestepping your own responsibility to "prove all things; hold fast that which is good" (1 Thess. 5:21).

5

Tools to Use

The principal tools that will prove useful in liberating a Mormon from his false beliefs fall into three main categories: (1) Christian literature critical of Mormonism, (2) Mormon scriptures including the Bible, and (3) other Mormon writings. To employ each effectively, it is necessary to understand how they can help your cause—or hurt if used incorrectly.

Christian Literature

In addition to the volume that you are presently reading there are many other books written by Christians to expose the errors of Mormonism. For instance, there is our previously mentioned *Mormons Answered Verse by Verse*, a quick-reference guide that discusses dozens of Bible passages Mormons misinterpret and suggests appropriate Christian responses. It also highlights Book of Mormon verses useful in discrediting the Book of Mormon. Read as many books like this as you can before your encounter to become familiar with the sect's history and beliefs. You will then be prepared for some of the off-the-wall arguments you can expect from well-trained LDS missionaries.

While such materials might beneficially be shared with someone starting to show an interest in the Latter-day Saints or just now commencing discussions with them, these books are best left unseen, and preferably unmentioned, to the full-fledged Mormon. The only books that you should bring to the table are the Bible itself and Mormon literature, which we will discuss shortly. (Your own hand-written notes are best kept on a small sheet of paper taped inside your Bible.)

The reason that other literature should be kept out of sight is threefold: (1) Literature exposing Mormonism may trigger a defensive response on the part of an LDS member who has been taught to see as persecution any efforts to expose the Church's errors. Defensive barriers immediately go up, and instead of your loved one thinking openmindedly about what you have to say, he or she begins to recite preprogramed responses to "persecution." (2) Having on hand material written by an "apostate" ex-Mormon would be almost as offensive as having such a person join you at the table. (3) It should be made clear that your faith and your beliefs are based on the Bible alone. This should stand out in sharp contrast to most Mormons, who place high confidence in the teachings of LDS Church leaders and teaching manuals published by the Mormon Church.

The Bible

When using Scripture in discussions with Mormons, it is important to keep in mind how they view the Bible and various translations.

First of all, the LDS Church has taught them to view the Bible as one of their *standard works* or scriptures. Why, then, is it so difficult to get a Mormon to see what the Bible says when it plainly refutes LDS doctrine? Why is it that a scriptural presentation that should reach a Mormon's heart appears to have little effect? Why do your biblical arguments fail to penetrate his or her thinking? The answer lies in his or her view of the Bible.

In the *Articles of Faith* Joseph Smith wrote, "We believe the Bible to be the word of God as far as it is translated correctly; we also believe the Book of Mormon to be the word of God" (Article Eight, Pearl of Great Price, 1990 edition, p. 60). But Mormons believe the Bible to be incomplete because the Book of Mormon states that "many parts" of the Bible are missing (1 Nephi 13:26–29). The implication of all this is that the Book of Mormon is more reliable than the Bible, and in fact Mormons do rely upon it and stress it as sacred scripture more so than the Bible. A May 22, 1992, open letter[1] from The First Presidency of the LDS Church declares, "The most reliable way to measure the accuracy of any biblical passage is not by comparing different texts, but by comparison with the Book of Mormon and modern-day revelations."

LDS Church leaders have acknowledged that they do not derive their teachings primarily from the Bible but that they *use* the Bible in persuading others to believe. Thus LeGrand Richards, one of the "general authorities" of the Church, concludes a doctrinal discussion in his book *A Marvelous Work And A Wonder* by saying: "The knowledge of all these things, as the reader will note, does not come to us primarily through reading the Bible, but through the revelations of the Lord in these latter days. We use the Bible to show that these teachings are completely in accord therewith" (1979 edition, p. 128).

The LDS Church publishes for the use of its members a King James Version Bible complete with a topical guide, a Bible dictionary, and extensive footnotes that cross reference Mormon writings. Included in the footnotes and in the appendix are excerpts from the *Joseph Smith Translation*—not actually a fresh translation but rather a revision of the King James Version that supposedly corrects errors, removes additions, and reinstates deletions that had crept into the text over the years. Joseph Smith made his "corrections" throughout the Bible not by consulting ancient manuscripts but through alleged divine inspiration. Strangely, though, the LDS Church has not formally canonized Smith's variations by including them in the text as sacred Scripture but has given them official sanction by including some of them in the footnotes and appendix of the Salt Lake City edition of the King James Bible. The Church has never published the complete "translation."

Smith's wife Emma refused to give the manuscript of the *Joseph Smith Translation* to her husband's successor, Brigham Young, but in 1866 she presented it to the Reorganized Church of Jesus Christ of Latter-Day Saints (RLDS), and that breakaway group published it the following year. In 1974 the LDS Church finally obtained

1. Published on page 3 of the LDS periodical *Church News,* June 20, 1992.

microfilm copies of the manuscript from the RLDS Church but has continued to hold back from publishing it—although the edition published by the RLDS Church is available at the LDS Deseret Book Store in Salt Lake City, where Mormons freely purchase it.

The *Joseph Smith Translation* apparently puts the Mormon leadership in somewhat of a dilemma. Some of Smith's revisions to the King James text fail to agree with the same passages as quoted in the Book of Mormon. Other portions contradict current Mormon doctrine. So, to fully endorse it could prove embarrassing. But to flatly reject it as erroneous would discredit Smith as a prophet. Instead, LDS leaders have sidestepped the issue by alleging that the work Smith began in 1831 was left unfinished at his death in 1844; that is, numerous errors remain in the uncorrected portions of the King James text, and, therefore, publication would be inappropriate. However, in a letter Smith wrote, dated July 2, 1833, at Kirtland, Ohio, he states that he "this day finished the translating of the Scriptures" (*History of the Church*, vol. 1, page 368).

In any case, Mormons today do use the King James Version Bible in discussions with Christians, citing it in support of LDS Church doctrines. In our book *Mormons Answered Verse by Verse* we demonstrate that those citations do not in fact support Mormon doctrine but that the Bible discredits both the doctrine and the other alleged "scriptures" of the LDS Church.

From all of the above information on how Mormons view the Bible it becomes clear why you cannot simply quote Scripture and reach the mind and heart of a fully indoctrinated LDS member. He or she never really looks at the Bible alone, without the guidance of other church publications. The Bible may be the only book on the table, but the Mormon keeps in mind his other writings that slant, color, contradict, or directly cancel out what a particular Bible verse says.

If you have never been a member of the sect, this may be difficult to grasp. It is hard to understand how someone can see a clear statement in the Bible, read it out loud, repeat it from memory, and still not get the point of what the verse says. Although LDS missionaries will tote their Bibles to your door and will read from Scripture to support their teachings, they are actually taking their instruction not from the Word of God but from Church publications that tell them what the Bible says and what it means. Likewise, when you show them a verse, have them read it, and ask them what it says, their response is governed by the prior indoctrination they have received rather than by what they have just read from the page.

To cope with this type of behavior, you must remember that more is happening than meets the eye. When you ask the individual to read a verse from the Bible, he or she reads it and then instantaneously does something else without your knowledge. The person's preprogramed mind automatically replaces what the verse says with the Church's interpretation of what it says. This is not a conscious dodge but rather a knee-jerk, or reflex, action that the Mormon may not even be aware of. Reading the verse triggers the official interpretation to pop up in the brain.

By being aware of what goes on in the Mormon's mind, you are in a better position to handle a biblical discussion. You will realize that it is not enough simply to read a verse and comment on it. Painstaking effort is necessary to get the LDS member to truly grasp what the verse says. The following steps are often helpful:

1. Rather than read the verse yourself, ask the Mormon to read it aloud from the Church's King James Bible. If you simply quote the verse from memory, the Mormon may assume that you misquoted it or, if you read it from a different translation, that it was mistranslated.

2. Have the Mormon break down the verse into clauses, phrases, and individual words. Ask him or her to comment on what each means. The LDS interpretation of the whole may disintegrate when the parts are examined separately.

3. Read the same verse from other recognized translations. A multiversion parallel Bible is helpful in this and can be obtained through a local Christian bookstore. The purpose of such a comparison would be not to discredit the King James Version but to avoid the word pattern that triggers recall of the preprogramed interpretation.

Mormon Scripture

The Church of Jesus Christ of Latter-day Saints refers to four volumes as the *standard works* of the Church, or canonized scripture: the Holy Bible (King James Version), the Book of Mormon,

Doctrine and Covenants, and Pearl of Great Price. All four are considered to be the word of God, and you would expect them to be in perfect harmony with one another. Actually, though, there is a great deal of doctrinal contradiction among these, and current Mormon doctrine can best be discerned from other sources such as teaching manuals published by the Mormon Church headquarters in Salt Lake City, talks by top Church leaders at official functions, Church magazines and newspapers, and books written by top LDS leaders through the Deseret Book Company in Salt Lake City. Since the top official of the Church is viewed as the living Prophet, with authority to speak for God, it is understandable that doctrine will vary over the years, with the current Prophet reinterpreting and overruling some earlier teachings. Bearing this in mind, here is a brief overview of the Mormon *standard works.*

Book of Mormon

Some eight million members of the Church of Jesus Christ of Latter-day Saints regard the Book of Mormon as a volume of Holy Scripture comparable to the Bible. They accept it as an inspired record of God's dealings with the inhabitants of the Americas, just as the Bible records his dealings with the Jews. Because the Book of Mormon includes accounts of alleged visits to America by the resurrected Christ, it contains elements similar to both the Old Testament and the New Testament of the Bible. Current editions add a subtitle so that the volume is labeled *The Book of Mormon: Another Testament of Jesus Christ.* This should call to mind the Bible's warning, "But though we, or an angel from heaven, preach any other gospel unto you than that which we have preached unto you, let him be accursed" (Gal. 1:8).

First published in 1830 in Palmyra, New York, the original edition says on its title page, "by Joseph Smith, Junior, author and proprietor." Current editions say, "translated by Joseph Smith, Jun."

Smith claimed that he was visited on September 21, 1823, by the angel Moroni, resurrected son of an ancient prophet-historian named Mormon who had written on gold plates quotations and abridgements of earlier writers Nephi, Jacob, Enos, *et al.* Before dying as the last of the Nephite people in A.D. 421, Moroni buried the gold plates in a stone vault on the Hill Cumorah, between what is now Palmyra and Manchester in western New York State. The angel took young Smith to the site in 1823 and let him unearth the stone vault and look into it but did not allow him to remove the gold plates until 1827. Then, along with the plates, Smith retrieved from the vault the Urim and Thummim—two stones set in silver bows, like eyeglasses, which enabled him miraculously to translate the "reformed Egyptian" characters written on the plates. After the translation work was completed, the angel Moroni reappeared and took back the plates.

So, unlike the books and epistles of the Bible that are attested to by literally thousands of ancient manuscripts such as the Dead Sea Scrolls that have been unearthed and preserved for inspection today, the Book of Mormon exists only as an English-language "translation" by one Joseph Smith. And, aside from the fact that his account of the angel and the golden plates is difficult for many to believe, there are other reasons to question the authenticity of the Book of Mormon.

One of these is Joseph Smith's personal background. Numerous reports from the period allege that he was a con man with a history of using a "peep stone" he put in his hat and then claimed it showed him where his clients might be successful in "money digging" or treasure hunting. Mormons respond that these charges surfaced when disgruntled ex-members of the Church began seeking ways to attack him. But public records establish that Joseph was brought to trial for such activities in Bainbridge, New York, on March 20, 1826, four years before he set up his Church and six years after he claimed to have been visited by God the Father and Jesus Christ. Official court documents refer to him as "Joseph Smith The Glass Looker." Moreover, writing about himself in the third person in his periodical *Elders' Journal*, Smith answered the question, "Was not Jo Smith a money digger?" by saying, "Yes, but it was never a very profitable job to him, as he only got fourteen dollars a month for it" (July 1838, p. 43).

Another problem revolves around allegations that Smith took much of the Book of Mormon from an unpublished novel titled *Manuscript Found*[2] by retired Congregational minister Solomon Spalding (1761–1816). Affadivits to that effect by Spalding's

2. Not to be confused with his other novel *Manuscript Story.*

widow, relatives, and neighbors were published in book form as *Mormonism Unvailed* by Eber D. Howe in 1834. Other material in the Book of Mormon closely parallels portions of *View of the Hebrews* by Ethan Smith (Poultney, Vermont, 1825). Ethan Smith was the Cowdery family's pastor in Poultney, Vermont, at the time Oliver Cowdery, Smith's scribe, left there in 1825. It is possible that Oliver had a copy of *View of the Hebrews.*

A number of books[3] have been and no doubt will continue to be written on the origin of the Book of Mormon.

LDS Apostle LeGrand Richards reports that Brigham Young's close associate Dr. Willard Richards made this remark after reading from the Book of Mormon for the first time: "That book was either written by God or the devil, and I am going to find out who wrote it."[4] Ten days later he concluded that it was from God. Many informed readers, however, have reached a different conclusion.

Doctrine and Covenants

Joseph Smith's first sixty-five "revelations" were published in 1833 as the *Book of Commandments for the Government of the Church of Christ.* This was revised and expanded in 1835 as the *Doctrine and Covenants of the Church of the Latter Day Saints.*[5] Today's version, 1990 printing, contains 138 sections plus two Official Declarations. Most of the sections are introduced as "revelations" given to Joseph Smith. Significant exceptions are section 135, which contains the official version of Smith's "martyrdom," and section 136 presented as "The Word and Will of the Lord, given through President Brigham Young." Sections 137 (Smith's "Vision of the Celestial Kingdom") and 138 (twentieth-century leader Joseph F. Smith's "Vision of the Redemption of the Dead") were officially added in 1979.

Unlike the much larger Book of Mormon, which consists mostly of purported history but which provides little in the way

3. See appendix 1.

4. *A Marvelous Work And A Wonder,* 1979 edition, p. 79.

5. This edition also contained a section called "Lectures of Faith," included in all editions until 1921 but then quietly removed without a "common consent" vote of the membership. The 1844 edition added seven revelations. In 1876, twenty-six additional revelations were added, many predated, having to do with priesthood authority. These were not voted on by "common consent" of the membership until October 1880.

of unique (nonbiblical) LDS Church doctrine, Doctrine and Covenants is full of instructions for the Church as to belief and practice. Concepts such as baptism for the dead, celestial marriage, priesthood, and polygamy are introduced and elaborated on. At the end of the 138 sections is Official Declaration-1 from LDS Church President Wilford Woodruff ending the practice[6] of polygamous marriage in 1890, and the 1978 Official Declaration-2 allowing black men to hold the priesthood.

Pearl of Great Price

This Mormon *standard work*, roughly sixty pages long in recent printings, is actually a collection of smaller writings: the *Book of Moses*, the *Book of Abraham*, portions from Joseph Smith's revision of Matthew's Gospel, Smith's account of his early visions and the golden plates, and the brief Mormon *Articles of Faith*.

The segment titled the *Book of Moses* is an elaboration and rewriting of the Book of Genesis. Copying much from the King James Version, it also adds some unique Mormon teachings. For example, it has Satan saying, "Behold, here I am, send me, I will be thy son, and I will redeem all mankind, that one soul shall not be lost, and surely I will do it . . . " (Moses 4:1). And the doctrine of spirit pre-existence before human birth is inserted: "And I, the Lord God, had created all the children of men; and not yet a man to till the ground; for in heaven created I them; and there was not yet flesh upon the earth . . . I made the world, and men before they were in the flesh" (Moses 3:5; 6:51). Moreover, Eve is made to say, "Were it not for our transgression, we should never have had seed." This claims that disobedience was necessary for human procreation (Moses 5:11). And Adam is told to be baptized in water in the name of the "Only Begotten Son . . . which is Jesus Christ," after which Adam goes on to be baptized and to be "born of the Spirit" thousands of years before Christ appeared on earth (Moses 6:52, 64–65).

The portion of Pearl of Great Price titled the *Book of Abraham* is unique in that it features three cuts or facsimiles of the Egyptian papyrus from which Joseph Smith allegedly "translated" it,

---

6. But the revelation approving plural marriage—Doctrine and Covenants 132—remains part of Mormon scripture.

with numbers keying the Egyptian symbols to explanatory notes below each cut. It is called, "The writings of Abraham while he was in Egypt, called the Book of Abraham, written by his own hand, upon papyrus."

This papyrus actually exists, having been seen in Smith's possession along with Egyptian mummies by many visitors, including reputable non-Mormons. But Smith's "translation" had to be miraculous, since he possessed no academic training in linguistics, and even trained Egyptologists were just beginning to discover how to decode Egyptian writing in his day. After being lost for some years and presumed destroyed, the papyrus was found in 1967 in New York's Metropolitan Museum and was identified by museum scholars and Mormon leaders as the same from which Smith had "translated" the *Book of Abraham.* It was examined and translated by experts, both Mormon and non-Mormon, in the now fully developed field of Egyptian writings. All of them concluded that the writings formed part of the "Book of Breathings," a pagan Egyptian funereal text totally unrelated to Abraham and that the correct translation bears no resemblance whatsoever to Joseph Smith's *Book of Abraham.*

In 1978, a dozen years after this major embarrassment, the LDS Church issued Official Declaration-2 dropping its longstanding ban on black men in the priesthood, without mentioning that the ban had been based largely on the now academically discredited *Book of Abraham* (1:21–26). Still, the book remains part of the Mormon *standard works* and a basis for other unique beliefs. It teaches, for example, the plurality of Gods: "And they went down at the beginning, and they, that is the Gods, organized and formed the heavens and the earth" (Abraham 4:1).

For a detailed study of the *Book of Abraham* see *By His Own Hand Upon Papyrus* listed in appendix 1.

Mormon Literature

The most powerful tool you can use to help a fully indoctrinated Mormon is his own literature. But how could that be so? Would not his own literature simply reinforce his existing beliefs? No, because it is here that you will find the documentary evidence disproving the LDS Church's claim to divine authority.

By looking at past teachings of the Church of Jesus Christ of Latter-day Saints and comparing them to present-day teaching, we find countless contradictions, false prophecies, and back-and-forth doctrinal changes. As we shall see in later chapters, Church leaders prophesied that the United States government would be overthrown in the 1800s, that the Civil War would fail to end black slavery, and that Utah would not gain statehood by abandoning polygamy. They have also reversed their teaching on the resurrection of children, changed their mind on whether God the Father has a body, taken contradictory positions on plural marriage, and even proclaimed the first man Adam to be God the Father. Yet, most Mormons either have no idea that some of these things happened, or they have read a vague, sugarcoated version.

For example, Mormons may read in their periodical *The Ensign* that certain detailed changes had been made to the Book of Mormon, but the changes covered are minor, and nothing is said about the major ones. When confronted with the facts on such matters, Mormons cannot help but be shocked (although most will try to hide their emotional upset or will express it as anger or frustration). And presented with one such shock after another, they cannot help but question their leaders' claims to speak for God.

The evidence is all right there, in black and white, in the pages of Mormon literature. Although encouraged not to read materials critical of their beliefs, Mormons can hardly refuse to look at their own literature. A few, in fact, maintain a personal library of the Church's publications for that very purpose and are accustomed to doing research and looking up information in these sources.

But it usually is not sufficient merely to quote the literature and to cite the publication, page, and paragraph. The Mormon will likely assume you misquoted it, or will favorably alter the quotation in his or her own mind and never bother to look it up for verification. The most effective approach is to produce a photocopy of the actual page, with the quotation highlighted, circled, or underlined in its original context. This cannot be dismissed as a baseless, hostile accusation. In fact, it is not your accusation that the Mormon must contend with but the LDS official spokesman's own words printed in the Church's own publications. Jesus said, "By thy words thou shalt be justified, and by thy words thou shalt be condemned" (Matt. 12:37), and the leaders of the Church of Jesus Christ of Latter-day Saints certainly have furnished more than enough evidence out of their own mouths to condemn it before God and man.

But even here you must exercise discernment as to when and how you will show these photocopies to a particular Mormon. Since the originals are not available to you and you are copying from a book such as ours, be sure to block out or cut off any added headings or page numbers, so that only the original LDS headings and page numbers remain. And then present them as "copies of Mormon literature," which they truly are, rather than mention that you got them second-hand from another book. (If the source of the photocopies becomes an issue, or if there are allegations that copies have been altered by anti-Mormons, neutral third-party photostats of original LDS materials can be obtained at your local public library through the interlibrary loan network.) Be sure to read the highlighted quotations aloud with your loved one and not just hand him or her a pile of papers in the hope that he or she will read them later on. But let the quotations themselves do most of the talking, rather than your repeated hammering on the point that the sect is false. After reading all the quotations in a calm, prayerful atmosphere, the Mormon will reach that conclusion himself, whether he admits it to you then or not.

Literature to Give the Mormon to Read

As pointed out above, literature that exposes Mormonism is best kept hidden from sight and unmentioned during discussions with LDS Church members. Eventually, however, if those discussions prove successful, the Mormon will want to start reading some outside material to further explore the organization's errors on his own. What should you recommend or give him to read? It should be something written with sensitivity to the Mormon reader in mind, such as *Mormons Answered Verse by Verse.* Another such book is *Why We Left Mormonism* by Latayne C. Scott (Baker Book House, 1990). The author is a former Brigham Young University scholarship student. She and seven other ex-members express themselves powerfully in their own words in this book. Additional books are listed under "Resources and Support Groups" in appendix 1. For information on materials not available through Christian bookstores you may contact Berean Christian Ministries, P.O. Box 1091, Webster, NY 14580 (enclose a business size, self-addressed stamped envelope).

6

Step-by-Step

If you have read and digested the preceding chapters, you are now ready to consider specific material to present to your Mormon friend or loved one. Ideally, this should be done step-by-step over a period of time. It takes time to program a person into a cultic mentality; so, likewise, it takes time to deprogram. Rushing the process can result in an aborted attempt—something that cannot be risked when there may be no opportunity for a second attempt.

The documentation assembled here could have a powerful impact on a Mormon or on an "investigator" receiving lessons from Mormon missionaries. It seems reasonable that no LDS Church member should be able to read these selections and simply shrug. Rather, he or she should find them extremely unsettling and giving rise to strong emotions and intense reevaluation of beliefs.

You should not expect to see an immediate outward manifestation of this except for, perhaps, an expression of anger or frustration. For a Mormon to express open disbelief in LDS teachings is to expose himself to censure and possible expulsion, so most members mask their inward questionings and hide their secret thoughts even from their most intimate associates. As the evidence you share with your Mormon friend begins to pile up, keep exercising patience. In some cases the information presented begins to have a subconscious effect before your friend becomes fully conscious of the implications. But, even when doubts mature to the point that they could be verbalized, he or she may not be ready to admit the mistake of falling for religious error. Such a mistake in judgment may be too embarrassing, at first, to admit to a non-Mormon. Or there may be fear of what Mormon friends will say. There may also be fear of official sanctions: losing the privilege of teaching or giving public talks; loss of the Temple Recommend; or even a warning from the bishop or stake president not to talk about certain issues that would undermine the faith of others. But when the Mormon is ready to talk about doubts, it will most likely be you who receives this confidence if you have shown yourself to be loving, caring, knowledgeable, and available for confidential talk.

It should also be noted that the Mormon exposed to the information we are about to present may react in several different ways. He may flee from the LDS Church and find Christ immediately. He may take refuge in the arms of his local bishop and resolve never again to critically examine his religion. Rather than go to either of these extremes, most take a more cautious course. Some remain in the Church but continue to wrestle with cherished beliefs and contradictory facts; some leave and find Christ only after wandering in the wilderness for a period; some leave the LDS Church but never find Christ.

We have seen different reactions in different individuals. Marriage mates may even respond differently. When evidence against the sect was presented eight years ago to one married couple, both active Mormons, the man left the Church, but his wife is still active in it eight years later. In another case a Christian man married a woman who told him she was a Mormon but did not say what she believed, and she had been attending a Christian church with him. After they were married, she renewed her interest in the Mormon Church and tried to get him into it. When he tried to show her why Mormonism was wrong, her response was to become more actively involved.

Whether a given individual will be liberated or further enslaved by an encounter with the truth will depend on a number of factors, some of which you cannot influence (for example, his or her personality and family circumstances) and some of which you can control (for example, your timing, approach, techniques, and personal example). Since the factors within your control may be enough to tip the balance one way or the other, it is imperative that you give due attention to the thoughts in our previous chapters on strategy, timing, techniques, and approach, as well as to the remaining chapters of this book. Applying these suggestions may mean the difference between success and failure. Moreover, since a bungled attempt may bar you from the opportunity to try again, you should muster all available resources to do it right the first time.

Rather than dispute various Mormon doctrinal beliefs one at a time, we have seen that the most effective strategy is one that takes aim at the LDS Church itself—the very basis for all of those false beliefs. "Is the Mormon Church truly what it claims to be?" That should be the focus of early discussions with a member, until he or she sees the sect for what it really is. After that, and only after that, can you successfully challenge the doctrinal beliefs that are now left to stand on their own without being upheld by the Prophet's authority. If the Church is what it claims to be, then all of its teachings must be true. But, if it is an impostor, then all of its teachings are suspect.

In brief, these are the steps you will need to take:

1. Document the claims made for itself by the Church of Jesus Christ of Latter-day Saints.

2. Disprove the Church's claims. Since it claims to be led by prophets, examine their prophecies to demonstrate that they are indeed false prophets. Since it claims to be the only true church, examine some of the ideas it has taught that are blatantly false.

3. Draw the conclusion that the LDS Church is not of God. At this point the Mormon's sense of obligation to the sect is greatly reduced or ends completely, and he or she is free to rethink beliefs and redirect life's goals and ambitions.

4. Establish the real truth of God. Help the new ex-Mormon fill the void in his or her life by getting to know God and coming into fellowship with genuine Christians.

5. Aid in deprograming and readjustment. It could take years for a fully indoctrinated Mormon to shed all the mental and emotional encumbrances acquired while in the sect. "It took me five months to accept Jesus, roughly another year or so to accept miscellaneous doctrines, and six years to formally join a church" (John

Farkas). The resources and ex-member support groups listed at the end of this book will prove helpful in this.

The next few chapters enable you first to establish the claims the LDS Church has made for itself and then to demonstrate the falsehood of those claims. To aid you in accomplishing this we provide documentation of statements found in Mormon literature, along with suggestions for discussing these with your deceived loved one. Bearing in mind that members are discouraged[1] from reading critical literature, it would be unwise to show them this book. Not only would many refuse to look at it, but they might also feel obliged to cease discussions with you since you are passing on to them "apostate" ideas. Instead, present the documents reproduced here as LDS literature, which they truly are and which Mormons should feel free to read.

1. For example, *Church News*, week ending June 6, 1992, p. 14, quoting Elder Carlos E. Asay of the Presidency of the Seventy: "Avoid those who would tear down your faith. . . . we place our souls in jeopardy when we receive the teachings of anyone except he that is ordained of God. . . . Do not contend or debate over points of doctrine." But see chapter 1, page 25 of this book for what past Mormon leaders have said. Why have they changed their thinking on this? Is it because they now know that Mormonism cannot stand the light?

7

Archaeology: Does It Support or Refute the Book of Mormon?

Your Mormon friend or loved one has been taught to believe that the Book of Mormon in its main story presents a history of the inhabitants of the Americas from about 600 B.C. to about A.D. 421. It tells not of a few nomadic Indians living in tepees but of Nephite and Lamanite nations—alleged descendants of Israel through his son Joseph—with huge populations living in fortified cities. Included is an alleged visit of Jesus Christ to these peoples in the New World shortly after his death in Jerusalem. It relates in detail how the Nephites and Lamanites waged large-scale wars with each other for centuries, culminating in a massive conflict in A.D. 385 in which hundreds of thousands[1] of people were killed near Hill Cumorah in present-day New York State (Mormon 6:9–15), where Joseph Smith allegedly unearthed the written record inscribed on golden plates. Did these nations really inhabit the Americas for a thousand years? If so, there should be an abundance of archaeological evidence.

Some idea of what to look for can be found by comparison with the Bible. Biblical archaeology is a major field of inquiry that has

---

1. The account at Mormon 6:9–15, 17–19 indicates at least 240,000 Nephite warriors killed, probably more, and assuming an equal number of Lamanites, we would have a total of at least 480,000 killed. Since the verses mention family members as accompanying them, the number of dead would be even higher.

filled museums with artifacts and has filled libraries with books on the cities, temples, fortresses, coins, inscriptions, and so on, that have been dug from mounds and ruins in Israel as well as in Lebanon, Syria, Egypt, Iran (Persia), Iraq (Babylon), and other lands mentioned in the Bible. Archaeologists have often used the Bible as a guide to what to look for and where, and the objects and writings uncovered have confirmed the Bible as factual, proving that the people and places spoken of in the Bible actually existed.

Ancient Egyptian and Babylonian records unearthed by archaeologists may portray their own pharaohs and kings as superior to the kings of Judah and Israel, but they thus verify the existence of those Jewish and gentile leaders named in the Bible. They may commemorate Egyptian and Babylonian victories over ancient Israel, while they ignore their own defeats, but they thus confirm that the battles really took place as recorded in the Bible. Can the same be said for the Book of Mormon?

Have archaeologists digging in North, South, and Central America used the Book of Mormon as a guide, as they have used the Bible in the Near and Middle East? Has the Book of Mormon guided them in locating and uncovering ruins of cities, temples, and fortifications mentioned in that book the way the Bible has? Have coins and inscriptions been unearthed in the Americas bearing the names of nations and rulers spoken of in the Book of Mormon, as excavations in Bible lands have uncovered references to Old Testament kings, New Testament Caesars, and even Pontius Pilate? And have any ancient writings been found in the Americas referring to the Book of Mormon's alleged appearances of Christ in this hemisphere, comparable to the nearly contemporary Roman and Jewish Talmud accounts, which refer to Jesus as a criminal and an impostor but at least acknowledge that he did walk the earth in first century A.D. Judea? What archaeological evidence is there for the Book of Mormon?

While apologists for the Mormon Church have written on the subject, and organizations have been formed by LDS members for the purpose of producing support for the Book of Mormon—with the result that Mormons are able to trot out alleged "proof" of its authenticity—there is an obvious difference between such chauvinistic efforts and the legitimate work of professional archaeologists. Thus, if LDS Church members choose to ignore the findings of the anthropology and archaeology departments of schools across the country in favor of conclusions reached at Brigham Young University, this should not be surprising. But anyone who approaches the subject with both eyes open quickly notices that Mormons keep citing Mormon sources for support, because support is lacking from academically recognized non-Mormon experts in the field.

Undoubtedly, one of the most comprehensive sources for historical and archaeological information on the Americas is the Smithsonian Institution in Washington, D.C. In 1990 we wrote to the Smithsonian Institution to inquire concerning the authenticity of the historical events portrayed in the Book of Mormon. Our letter asked these specific questions:

1. Is the Book of Mormon used to find archaeological sites in the New World?
2. Is there archaeological evidence that prior to the European influence, the North, Central and South American Indians did:
   a. use iron and/or steel?
   b. use vehicles with wheels like full size wagons, carts, chariots or similar?
   c. use or have access to asses, goats, horses, sheep, elephants, cattle, oxen, cows?
   d. use or have access to domesticated plants like wheat, barley, oats, millet and rice?
   e. use silk or linen?
3. Did some or all of the original ancestors of the American Indians come from Israel or some Semitic family?
4. Have any New World archaeological sites ever been connected to a Book of Mormon event or location? If so, please name them.

Aside from the broad questions involving archaeological sites and ethnic origins, the specific items we asked about were based on Book of Mormon references to iron (2 Nephi 5:15; 20:34; Jarom 1:8; Mosiah 11:8; Ether 10:23); steel (1 Nephi 4:9; 16:18; 2 Nephi 5:15; Ether 7:9); vehicles with wheels (Alma 18:9–10, 12; 3 Nephi 3:22; 21:14); asses (1 Nephi 18:25; Mosiah 5:14; 12:5; Ether 9:19);

goats (1 Nephi 18:25; Alma 14:29; Ether 9:18); horses (1 Nephi 18:25; 2 Nephi 12:7; Enos 1:21; Alma 18:9–12; 3 Nephi 3:22; 21:14; Ether 9:19); sheep (Ether 9:18); elephants (Ether 9:19); cattle (Enos 1:21; 3 Nephi 3:22; 6:1; Ether 9:18); oxen (1 Nephi 18:25; Ether 9:18); cows (1 Nephi 18:25; Ether 9:18); wheat (Mosiah 9:9); grain (Helaman 11:17); silk (1 Nephi 13:7; Alma 1:29; Ether 9:17); and linen (1 Nephi 13:7–8; Mosiah 10:5; Alma 1:29; 4:6; Ether 10:24).

Apparently we were not the first to make such an inquiry. The Smithsonian's Public Inquiry Mail Service responded with a brief cover letter addressed to John R. Farkas and dated January 26, 1990, accompanied by printed form letters on the subject in question. (See photostats of these documents at the end of this chapter.) The form letters took a much stronger tone than we would have expected. The first one, on stationery of the Smithsonian's National Museum of Natural History, said this:

> Your recent inquiry concerning the Smithsonian Institution's alleged use of the Book of Mormon as a scientific guide has been received in the Smithsonian's Department of Anthropology.
>
> The Book of Mormon is a religious document and not a scientific guide. The Smithsonian Institution has never used it in archaeological research and any information that you have received to the contrary is incorrect. Accurate information about the Smithsonian's position is contained in the enclosed "Statement Regarding the Book of Mormon," which was prepared to respond to the numerous inquiries that the Smithsonian receives on this topic.
>
> Because the Smithsonian regards the unauthorized use of its name to disseminate inaccurate information as unlawful, we would appreciate your assistance in providing us with the names of any individuals who are misusing the Smithsonian's name. Please address any correspondence to:
>
> Public Information Officer
> Department of Anthropology
> National Museum of Natural History
> Smithsonian Institution
> Washington, DC 20560
>
> PREPARED BY
> THE DEPARTMENT OF ANTHROPOLOGY
> SMITHSONIAN INSTITUTION

It would appear that this form letter was aimed at combating misinformation relating to the Smithsonian itself, rather than simply answering questions such as those in our letter. The official "Statement Regarding the Book of Mormon" reads as follows:

1. The Smithsonian Institution has never used the Book of Mormon in any way as a scientific guide. Smithsonian archaeologists see no direct connection between the archaeology of the New World and the subject matter of the book.

2. The physical type of the American Indian is basically Mongoloid, being most closely related to that of the peoples of eastern, central, and northeastern Asia. Archaeological evidence indicates that the ancestors of the present Indians came into the New World— probably over a land bridge known to have existed in the Bering Strait region during the last Ice Age—in a continuing series of small migrations beginning from about 25,000 to 30,000 years ago.

3. Present evidence indicates that the first people to reach this continent from the East were the Norsemen who briefly visited the northeastern part of North America around A.D. 1000 and then settled in Greenland. There is nothing to show that they reached Mexico or Central America.

4. One of the main lines of evidence supporting the scientific finding that contacts with Old World civilizations, if indeed they occurred at all, were of very little significance for the development of American Indian civilizations, is the fact that none of the principal Old World domesticated food plants or animals (except the dog) occurred in the New World in pre-Columbian times. American Indians had no wheat, barley, oats, millet, rice, cattle, pigs, chickens, horses, donkeys, camels before 1492. (Camels and horses were in the Americas, along with the bison, mammoth, and mastodon, but all these animals became extinct around 10,000 B.C. at the time when the early big-game hunters spread across the Americas.)

5. Iron, steel, glass, and silk were not used in the New World before 1492 (except for occasional use of unsmelted meteoric iron). Native copper was worked in various locations in pre-Columbian times, but true metallurgy was limited to southern Mexico and the Andean region, where its occurrence in late prehistoric times involved gold, silver, copper, and their alloys, but not iron. [Note: This precludes steel.—*authors*]

6. There is a possibility that the spread of cultural traits across the Pacific to Mesoamerica and the northwestern coast of South

America began several hundred years before the Christian era. However, any such inter-hemisphere contacts appear to have been the results of accidental voyages originating in eastern and southern Asia. It is by no means certain that even such contacts occurred; certainly there were no contacts with the ancient Egyptians, Hebrews, or other peoples of Western Asian [sic] and the Near East.

7. No reputable Egyptologist or other specialist on Old World archaeology, and no expert on New World prehistory, has discovered or confirmed any relationship between archaeological remains in Mexico and archaeological remains in Egypt.

8. Reports of findings of ancient Egyptian, Hebrew, and other Old World writings in the New World in pre-Columbian contexts have frequently appeared in newspapers, magazines, and sensational books. None of these claims has stood up to examination by reputable scholars. No inscriptions using Old World forms of writing have been shown to have occurred in any part of the Americas before 1492 except for a few Norse rune stones which have been found in Greenland.

So, while archaeologists working in the Near East and the Middle East have found an abundance of artifacts confirming the history found in the Bible, what archaeologists have found in the Americas fails to support the Book of Mormon and, in fact, contradicts it.

Both Mormon founder Joseph Smith, Jr., and current LDS Church President Ezra Taft Benson have called the Book of Mormon "the keystone of our religion."[2] The archaeological evidence against the Book of Mormon, then, serves as evidence also against the entire Church of Jesus Christ of Latter-day Saints.

2. *The Ensign*, January, 1992, pp. 2–5.

BEREAN
CHRISTIAN
MINISTRIES

John R. Farkas, President
Phyllis Farkas, Co-Worker

(ACTS 17:10-11) *"these were more noble . . . and searched the scriptures daily whether those things were so."*

January 1, 1990

Smithsonian Institution
National Museum of Natural History
Washington, D.C. 20560

Dear Sir or Madam:

I have been reading the Book of Mormon, a scripture of "The Church of Jesus Christ of Latter-day Saints" (the Mormons). I have questions concerning the authenticity of the historical events that it portrays. They are:

1. Is the Book of Mormon used to find archaelological sites in the New World?

2. Is there archaeological evidence that prior to the European influence, the North, Central and South American Indians did:

   a. use iron and or steel?
   b. use vehicles with wheels like full size wagons, carts, chariots or similar?
   c. use or have access to asses, goats, horses, sheep, elephants, cattle, oxen, cows?
   d. use or have access to domesticated plants like wheat, barley, oats, millet and rice?
   e. use silk and or linen?

3. Did some or all of the original ancestors of the American Indians come from Israel or some Semitic family?

4. Have any New World archaeological sites ever been connected to a Book of Mormon event or location? If so, please name them.

Thank you for your response to the above and any related information you may wish to send. I have enclosed a check for $2.00 to cover postage, handling etc.

Sincerely yours,

John R. Farkas

John R. Farkas

Letter to the Smithsonian Institution.

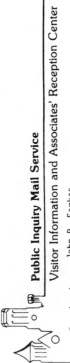

Public Inquiry Mail Service

Visitor Information and Associates' Reception Center

Speed reply to   John R. Farkas

Date January 26, 1990

Your recent inquiry has been received in this office for response.

Enclosed please find material which we trust will prove helpful.

Thank you for your interest in the Smithsonian Institution.

P.S. Your check is returned herewith.

12/88C

Smithsonian Institution   Washington, DC 20560

Smithsonian Institution's cover letter.

Information from the

National Museum of Natural History

SMITHSONIAN INSTITUTION   WASHINGTON, D.C. 20560

Your recent inquiry concerning the Smithsonian Institution's alleged use of the Book of Mormon as a scientific guide has been received in the Smithsonian's Department of Anthropology.

The Book of Mormon is a religious document and not a scientific guide. The Smithsonian Institution has never used it in archeological research and any information that you have received to the contrary is incorrect. Accurate information about the Smithsonian's position is contained in the enclosed "Statement Regarding the Book of Mormon," which was prepared to respond to the numerous inquiries that the Smithsonian receives on this topic.

Because the Smithsonian regards the unauthorized use of its name to disseminate inaccurate information as unlawful, we would appreciate your assistance in providing us with the names of any individuals who are misusing the Smithsonian's name. Please address any correspondence to:

> Public Information Officer
> Department of Anthropology
> National Museum of Natural History
> Smithsonian Institution
> Washington, DC 20560

PREPARED BY
THE DEPARTMENT OF ANTHROPOLOGY
SMITHSONIAN INSTITUTION

Smithsonian Institution's form letter on Book of Mormon.
Used with permission.

STATEMENT REGARDING THE BOOK OF MORMON

1. The Smithsonian Institution has never used the Book of
Mormon in any way as a scientific guide. Smithsonian
archeologists see no direct connection between the archeology
of the New World and the subject matter of the book.

2. The physical type of the American Indian is basically
Mongoloid, being most closely related to that of the peoples
of eastern, central, and northeastern Asia. Archeological
evidence indicates that the ancestors of the present Indians
came into the New World--probably over a land bridge known to
have existed in the Bering Strait region during the last Ice
Age--in a continuing series of small migrations beginning
from about 25,000 to 30,000 years ago.

3. Present evidence indicates that the first people to reach
this continent from the East were the Norsemen who briefly
visited the northeastern part of North America around A.D.
1000 and then settled in Greenland. There is nothing to show
that they reached Mexico or Central America.

4. One of the main lines of evidence supporting the
scientific finding that contacts with Old World
civilizations, if indeed they occurred at all, were of very
little significance for the development of American Indian
civilizations, is the fact that none of the principal Old
World domesticated food plants or animals (except the dog)
occurred in the New World in pre-Columbian times. American
Indians had no wheat, barley, oats, millet, rice, cattle,
pigs, chickens, horses, donkeys, camels before 1492. (Camels
and horses were in the Americas, along with the bison,
mammoth, and mastodon, but all these animals became extinct
around 10,000 B.C. at the time when the early big game
hunters spread across the Americas.)

SIL-76
1988

5. Iron, steel, glass, and silk were not used in the New World before 1492 (except for occasional use of unsmelted meteoric iron). Native copper was worked in various locations in pre-Columbian times, but true metallurgy was limited to southern Mexico and the Andean region, where its occurrence in late prehistoric times involved gold, silver, copper, and their alloys, but not iron.

6. There is a possibility that the spread of cultural traits across the Pacific to Mesoamerica and the northwestern coast of South America began several hundred years before the Christian era. However, any such inter-hemispheric contacts appear to have been the results of accidental voyages originating in eastern and southern Asia. It is by no means certain that even such contacts occurred; certainly there were no contacts with the ancient Egyptians, Hebrews, or other peoples of Western Asian and the Near East.

7. No reputable Egyptologist or other specialist on Old World archeology, and no expert on New World prehistory, has discovered or confirmed any relationship between archeological remains in Mexico and archeological remains in Egypt.

8. Reports of findings of ancient Egyptian, Hebrew, and other Old World writings in the New World in pre-Columbian contexts have frequently appeared in newspapers, magazines, and sensational books. None of these claims has stood up to examination by reputable scholars. No inscriptions using Old World forms of writing have been shown to have occurred in any part of the Americas before 1492 except for a few Norse rune stones which have been found in Greenland.

Smithsonian Institution's "Statement Regarding the Book of Mormon." Used with permission.

8

Gods and Goddesses

Anyone listening to the Mormon Tabernacle Choir sing sacred Christmas music would automatically assume that Mormons espouse essentially the same theology as traditional Christian churches. And this, apparently, is the image the LDS Church's public relations people try to project. But, in fact, nothing could be farther from the truth. While knowledgeable Mormons may be familiar with their Church's unique theology, newer members and individuals in the process of joining may find the facts shocking. Presenting this information to a loved one in the early stages of his or her involvement may be all that is needed to terminate the missionaries' visits.

Although the Bible teaches that Almighty God is "from everlasting to everlasting" (Ps. 90:2) and is "the only true God" (John 17:3) because "there is but one God" (1 Cor. 8:6), Mormonism teaches that God the Father was once a mortal man like us, that he progressed to become a God, and that we, too, by adopting and faithfully adhering to Mormonism, can become Gods like him. In fact, the LDS Church teaches that there are already many Gods. Among these is our heavenly Father and also his wife, our heavenly Mother. In fact, God the Father is said to have a father, a grandfather, and so on. Thus, Mormonism bears little resemblance to Judeo-Christian monotheism; rather, it is closer to the polytheism of the ancient Greeks and Romans who pictured a whole pantheon of gods and goddesses cavorting on Mount Olympus procreating divine children.

Moreover, despite the many Bible-based Christmas hymns sung by the Mormon Tabernacle Choir, the LDS Church teaches that God the Father, who has a body of flesh and bones in form like a man, came down and visited the Virgin Mary to get her pregnant not by the Holy Spirit but personally in the same way mortal men father their children. This is what Mormon publications have in mind when they refer to Jesus as "the Only Begotten of the Father."

Shocking indeed! But does the foregoing accurately sum up the official teaching of the Church of Jesus Christ of Latter-day Saints? Yes. These teachings can be found in numerous LDS publications, although not in those normally given to outsiders or to people interested in joining the sect. For example, founder Joseph Smith taught this on April 6, 1844, at a Church conference:

> In the beginning, the head of the Gods called a council of the Gods; and they came together and concocted a plan to create the world and people it (*Journal of Discourses* 6:5; *Teachings of the Prophet Joseph Smith*, p. 349; and *History of the Church*, vol. 6, p. 308).

The 1976 student manual *Achieving a Celestial Marriage*, published by the Corporation of the President of The Church of Jesus Christ of Latter-day Saints, proclaims the following:

> . . . God is an exalted man who once lived on an earth and underwent experiences of mortality. His marriage partner is our mother in heaven. . . . GOD WAS ONCE A MORTAL MAN [section heading]. . . . He Lived on an Earth like Our Own . . . (p. 129).

> As shown in this chapter, our Father in heaven was once a man as we are now, capable of physical death. By obedience to eternal gospel principles, he progressed from one stage of life to another until he attained the state that we call exaltation or godhood. In such a condition, he and our mother in heaven were empowered to give birth to spirit children . . . (p. 132).

This manual quotes numerous past leaders such as Brigham Young and Joseph F. Smith to establish these teachings as official church doctrine. For example, concerning our alleged potential to achieve "exaltation" as Gods ourselves, it quotes "Smith, *Teachings*, pp. 346–48" as follows:

> . . . you have got to learn how to be Gods yourselves, and to be kings and priests to God, the same as all Gods have done before you, namely, by going from one small degree to another . . . (p. 130).

The current textbook *Gospel Principles*, 1986 edition, also published by the Corporation of the President of The Church of Jesus Christ of Latter-day Saints, confirms this teaching:

> We can become Gods like our Heavenly Father. This is exaltation.
>
> . . . .
>
> (2) They will become gods.
> (3) They will have their righteous family members with them and will be able to have spirit children also. These spirit children will have the same relationship to them as we do to our Heavenly Father. They will be an eternal family (p. 290).

History of the Church 6:476 presents this line of reasoning:

> . . . If Jesus Christ was the Son of God, and John discovered that God the Father of Jesus Christ had a Father, you may suppose that He had a Father also. Where was there ever a son without a father?
> . . . Hence if Jesus had a Father, can we not believe that *He* had a Father also? I despise the idea of being scared to death at such a doctrine, for the Bible is full of it.

Elsewhere, *Teachings of the Prophet Joseph Smith* compiled by Joseph Fielding Smith[1] declares that ". . . God the Father of Jesus Christ had a Father, and that you may suppose that He had a Father also." The teaching, "The Father has a body of flesh and bones as tangible as man's," is found in Doctrine and Covenants 130:22, part of LDS scripture.

Although the Bible informs us that Jesus was born of "a virgin" (Luke 1:27), Mormonism teaches otherwise. The Bible says Mary was engaged to marry Joseph, but "before they came together, she was found with child of the Holy Ghost" (Matt. 1:18). Prophet

---

1. (Salt Lake City: Deseret Book Co., 1976 ed.) p. 373.

Brigham Young, however, taught that "our God has a body, parts, and passions"2 and that "the Father came down from heaven . . . and begat the Saviour of the world; for he is the ONLY-begotten of the Father, which could not be if the Father did not actually beget him in person." What did Brigham Young mean by "in person"? He interrupted himself here in this discourse with a rhetorical objection by a fictitious non-Mormon saying, "I cannot believe that, for he is a God without body, parts, or passions," and then answered the objection by declaring, "I believe the Father came down in His tabernacle [body in Mormon terminology] and begat Jesus Christ."3

Speaking on another occasion, Brigham Young clarified his position this way:4

> The birth of the Saviour was as natural as are the births of our children; it was the result of natural action. He partook of flesh and blood—was begotten of his Father, as we were of our fathers.

The book *Mormon Doctrine*5 explains it this way:

> ONLY BEGOTTEN SON . . . These name-titles all signify that our Lord is the only Son of the Father in the flesh. Each of the words is to be understood literally. Only means *only*; Begotten means *begotten*; and Son means *son*. Christ was begotten by an Immortal Father in the same way that mortal men are begotten by mortal fathers (pp. 546–47).

And *Family Home Evening*,6 a teaching manual published by the Mormon Church to guide member families, puts it in simpler terms for children to understand:

---

2. Brigham Young, October 7, 1857, *Journal of Discourses* 5:331.

3. Brigham Young, July 24, 1853, *Journal of Discourses* 1:238. Note that this was delivered at a General Conference. Such a meeting is held twice each year in April and October. The top leaders of the LDS Church address the general membership with important items of instruction over a three-day period. They do not speak on casual subjects or present personal opinions. So we have here the President and Prophet of the Mormon Church teaching this at an official Mormon Church meeting. It is not personal opinion or speculation; he requires the total Mormon Church membership to accept it.

4. Brigham Young, July 8, 1860, *Journal of Discourses* 8:115.

5. Mormon Apostle Bruce R. McConkie, *Mormon Doctrine* (Bookcraft, 1966; 2nd edition, 1979).

6. *Family Home Evening* (Corporation of the President of The Church of Jesus Christ of Latter-day Saints, 1972 edition) Lesson 27, "Whom Say Ye that I Am," pp. 125–26.

... I am going to tell you a simple truth ... one of the greatest truths ... most simple fact ever revealed. ... Jesus Christ is the only begotten Son of God in the flesh. Well, now for the benefit of the older ones, how are children begotten? I answer just as Jesus Christ was begotten of his father (p. 125). [The manual here shows these are the words of Joseph F. Smith, then the President and Prophet of the Mormon Church, speaking in 1914 at an official church meeting.]

According to Mormonism all of us humans lived as spirits before we received *tabernacles* [bodies] of flesh; the Heavenly Father and Heavenly Mother produced our spirits, and then later our earthly parents procreated our tabernacles [bodies]. With this in mind, note how Brigham Young explained God's role in Jesus' conception:

When the time came that His first-born, the Saviour, should come into the world and take a tabernacle, the Father came Himself and favoured that spirit with a tabernacle instead of letting any other man do it. The Saviour was begotten by the Father of His spirit, by the same Being who is the Father of our spirits, and that is all the organic difference between Jesus Christ and you and me.[7]

In words reminiscent of the pagan Greek myth of Hercules, son of the god Zeus and a mortal woman, the current 1988 edition of the book *Articles of Faith*, by James E. Talmage, cites an official teaching from "The First Presidency and the Council of the Twelve Apostles of the Church of Jesus Christ of Latter-day Saints" concerning Christ's "unique status in the flesh as the offspring of a mortal mother and of an immortal, or resurrected and glorified, Father" (p. 473). The Mormon Sunday school textbook *Messages for Exaltation* uses italics to convey the same point when it quotes Church President David O. McKay teaching at a Church conference in 1966: "The Man of Galilee is—not figuratively, but *literally*—the Son of the living God."[8] And current President Ezra Taft Benson has written this:

7. Brigham Young, February 8, 1857, *Journal of Discourses* 4:218.
8. Anonymous (Salt Lake City: Deseret Sunday School Union, 1967), p. 111.

[There is] no question as to the paternity of Jesus Christ. God was the Father of Jesus' mortal tabernacle, and Mary, a mortal woman, was His mother.... The Church of Jesus Christ of Latter-day Saints proclaims that Jesus Christ is the Son of God in the most literal sense. The body in which He performed His mission in the flesh was sired by that same Holy Being we worship as God, our Eternal Father. Jesus was not the son of Joseph, nor was He begotten by the Holy Ghost.... He was the Only Begotten Son of our Heavenly Father in the flesh—the only child whose mortal body was begotten by our Heavenly Father.[9]

This belief that the fleshly body of Jesus Christ was conceived through an ordinary physical act of procreation between God the Father and the Virgin Mary is thus confirmed as a longstanding teaching of the LDS Church, presented as "one of the greatest truths," and endorsed in the above quotations by two of its prophets, two Mormon apostles, and official Church publications dating from 1857 through the present.

Beyond this, Mormon leaders have even taught that Jesus himself traveled about "with a train of women, such as used to follow him, fondling about him, combing his hair," and the following:

... there was a marriage in Cana of Galilee; and on a careful reading of that transaction, it will be discovered that no less a person than Jesus Christ was married on that occasion. If he was never married, his intimacy with Mary and Martha, and the other Mary also whom Jesus loved, must have been highly unbecoming and improper to say the best of it (President Orson Hyde, speaking at Great Salt Lake, no date, *Journal of Discourses* 4:259).

Orson Pratt writing in *The Seer* (October 1853) makes the same point: "If all the acts of Jesus were written, we no doubt should learn that these beloved women were his wives" (p. 159). Speaking on March 18, 1855, LDS General Authority Orson Hyde added that Jesus also fathered children by these women:

... I said, in my lecture on Marriage, at our last Conference, that Jesus Christ was married at Cana of Galilee, that Mary, Martha,

9. Ezra Taft Benson, *The Teachings of Ezra Taft Benson* (Salt Lake City: Bookcraft, 1988), p. 7.

and others were his wives, and that he begat children (Orson Hyde, March 18, 1855, *Journal of Discourses*, 2:210).

This Mormon theology involving multiple gods and goddesses, with Jesus Christ and God the Father portrayed as married and fathering offspring, is totally foreign to those who derive their religious beliefs from the Bible alone. Rather, as stated at the beginning of this chapter, it does indeed recall the lustful polytheism of Greece and Rome. If people investigating Mormonism, and even new LDS members, can be shown that the church's teachings eventually lead to such shocking nonbiblical ideas as these, this may result in their rethinking their involvement. Many who understand God and Christ as the Bible presents them will find Mormon theology offensive. (Discussions in *Mormons Answered Verse by Verse* may prove helpful in establishing the biblical view.) It is likely that even unchurched people will recognize Mormon theology as foreign to the thinking of nominally Christian society. At the very least, lovers of truth will note an element of deceptiveness in marketing Mormonism without clearly labeling it "polytheism" on the outside of the package.

than what I have told you. Thus, the head God brought forth the Gods in the grand council.

I will transpose and simplify it in the English language. Oh, ye lawyers, ye doctors, and ye priests, who have persecuted me, I want to let you know that the Holy Ghost knows something as well as you do. The head God called together the Gods and sat in grand council to bring forth the world. The grand counsellors sat at the head in yonder heavens, and contemplated the creation of the worlds which were created at that time. When I say doctors and lawyers, I mean the doctors and lawyers of the Scriptures. I have done so hitherto without explanation, to let the lawyers flutter, and everybody laugh at them. Some learned doctor might take a notion to say the Scriptures say thus and so; and we must believe the Scriptures; they are not to be altered. But I am going to show you an error in them.

I have an old edition of the New Testament in the Hebrew, Latin, German, and Greek languages. I have been reading the German, and find it to be the most correct translation, and to correspond nearest to the revelations which God has given to me for the last fourteen years. It tells about Jachoboy, the son of Zebedee. It means Jacob. In the English New Testament it is translated James. Now, if Jacob had the keys, you might talk about James through all eternity, and never get the keys. In the 21st verse of the fourth chapter of Matthew, my old German edition gives the word Jacob instead of James.

The doctors (I mean doctors of law, not of physic,) say, " If you preach anything not according to the Bible, we will cry treason." How can we escape the damnation of hell, except God be with us and reveal to us? Men bind us with chains. The Latin says Jachabod, which means Jacob;

the Hebrew says Jacob, the Greek says Jacob, and the German says Jacob. Here we have the testimony of four against one. I thank God I have got this old book; but I thank him more for the gift of the Holy Ghost. I have got the oldest book in the world; but I have got the oldest book in my heart, even the gift of the Holy Ghost. I have all the four Testaments. Come here, ye learned men, and read, if you can. I should not have introduced this testimony, were it not to back up the word *Rosh*— the head, the father of the Gods. I should not have brought it up, only to show that I am right.

In the beginning, the head of the Gods called a council of the Gods; and they came together and concocted a plan to create the world and people it. When we begin to learn in this way, we begin to learn the only true God and what kind of a being we have got to worship. Having a knowledge of God, we begin to know how to approach him and how to ask so as to receive an answer.

When we understand the character of God and know how to come to him, he begins to unfold the heavens to us and to tell us all about it. When we are ready to come to him, he is ready to come to us.

Now, I ask all who hear me, why the learned men who are preaching salvation say that God created the heavens and the earth out of nothing? The reason is, that they are unlearned in the things of God and have not the gift of the Holy Ghost. They account it blasphemy in any one to contradict their idea. If you tell them that God made the world out of something, they will call you a fool. But I am learned, and know more than all the world put together. The Holy Ghost does, anyhow; and he is within me, and comprehends more than all the world; and I will associate myself with him.

Celestial Marriage: Key to Exaltation

(1-1) INTRODUCTION

The gospel of Jesus Christ teaches that man is an eternal being, made in the image and likeness of God. It also holds that man is a literal child of God and has the potential, if faithful to divine laws and ordinances, of becoming like his heavenly parent. These truths are generally well understood by Latter-day Saints.

Less well understood, however, is the fact that God is an exalted man who once lived on an earth and underwent experiences of mortality. The Prophet Joseph Smith refers to this as "the great secret." (*Times and Seasons* 5:613 [15 Aug. 1844]. See also Joseph Smith, *Teachings of the Prophet Joseph Smith*, p. 345.) The progression of our Father in heaven to godhood, or exaltation, was strictly in accordance with eternal principles, "for he who is not able to abide the law of a celestial kingdom cannot abide a celestial glory." (D&C 88:22.)

By definition, exaltation includes the ability to procreate the family unit throughout eternity. This our Father in heaven has power to do. His marriage partner is our mother in heaven. We are their spirit children, born to them in the bonds of celestial marriage.

The Lord would have all his children attain exaltation, but men must have their agency. Only those who subscribe by ordinance and by faithful adherence to covenant are worthy of "a continuation of the seeds forever and ever." (D&C 132:19.)

GOD WAS ONCE A MORTAL MAN

(1-2) He Lived on an Earth like Our Own

"God himself was once as we are now, and is an exalted man, and sits enthroned in yonder heavens! That is the great secret. If the veil were rent today, and the great God who holds this world in its orbit and who upholds all worlds and all things by his power was to make himself visible,—I say, if you were to see him today, you would see him like a man in form—like yourselves in all the person, image, and very form as a man; for Adam was created in the very fashion, image and likeness of God and received instruction from, and walked, talked and conversed with him, as one man talks and communes with another." (Smith, *Teachings*, p. 345.)

Achieving a Celestial Marriage, p. 129. Copyright © 1976 Corporation of the President of The Church of Jesus Christ of Latter-day Saints.

(1-20) SUMMARY

As shown in this chapter, our Father in heaven was once a man as we are now, capable of physical death. By obedience to eternal gospel principles, he progressed from one stage of life to another until he attained the state that we call exaltation or godhood. In such a condition, he and our mother in heaven were empowered to give birth to spirit children whose potential was equal to that of their heavenly parents. We are those spirit children.

Achieving a Celestial Marriage, p. 132. Copyright © 1976 Corporation of the President of The Church of Jesus Christ of Latter-day Saints.

edge and all wisdom. He is the father of spirit children. He is a creator. We can become Gods like our Heavenly Father. This is exaltation.

If we prove faithful and obedient to all the commandments of the Lord, we will live in the highest degree of the celestial kingdom of heaven. We will become exalted, just like our Heavenly Father. Exaltation is the highest reward that our Heavenly Father can give his children. The Lord has said that exaltation is the greatest gift of all the gifts of God (see D&C 14:7).

What is exaltation?

BLESSINGS OF EXALTATION

Our Heavenly Father is perfect. However, he is not jealous of his wisdom and perfection. He glories in the fact that it is possible for his children to become like him. He has said: "This is my work and my glory—to bring to pass the immortality and eternal life of man" (Moses 1:39).

Those who live the commandments of the Lord and receive eternal life (exaltation) in the celestial kingdom will receive special blessings. The Lord has said: "All [things] are theirs" (D&C 76:59). These are some of the special blessings given to exalted persons:

1. They will live eternally in the presence of our Heavenly Father and Jesus Christ (see D&C 76).

2. They will become gods.

3. They will have their righteous family members with them and will be able to have spirit children also. These spirit children will have the same relationship to them as we do to our Heavenly Father. They will be an eternal family.

4. They will receive a fullness of joy.

5. They will have everything that our Heavenly Father and Jesus Christ have, all power, glory, dominion, and knowledge. President Joseph Fielding Smith wrote: "The Father has promised through the Son that all that he has shall be given to those who are obedient to his commandments. *They*

Gospel Principles, 1985 edition, p. 290. Copyright © 1978, 1979, 1981 Corporation of the President of The Church of Jesus Christ of Latter-day Saints.

In the very beginning the Bible shows there is a plurality of Gods beyond the power of refutation. It is a great subject I am dwelling on. The word *Eloheim* ought to be in the plural all the way through— Gods. The heads of the Gods appointed one God for us; and when you take [that] view of the subject, it sets one free to see all the beauty, holiness and perfection of the Gods. All I want is to get the simple, naked truth, and the whole truth.

Many men say there is one God; the Father, the Son and the Holy Ghost are only one God! I say that is a strange God anyhow—three in one, and one in three! It is a curious organization. "Father, I pray not for the world, but I pray for them which thou hast given me." "Holy Father, keep through Thine own name those whom thou hast given me, that they may be one as we are." All are to be crammed into one God, according to sectarianism. It would make the biggest God in all the world. He would be a wonderfully big God—he would be a giant or a monster. I want to read the text to you myself—"I am agreed with the Father and the Father is agreed with me, and we are agreed as one." The Greek shows that it should be agreed. "Father, I pray for them which Thou hast given me out of the world, and not for those alone, but for them also which shall believe on me through their word, that they all may be agreed, as Thou, Father, art with me, and I with Thee, that they also may be agreed with us," and all come to dwell in unity, and in all the glory and everlasting burnings of the Gods; and then we shall see as we are seen, and be as our God and He as His Father. I want to reason a little on this subject. I learned it by trans- lating the papyrus which is now in my house. I learned a testimony concerning Abraham, and he reasoned concerning the God of heaven. "In order to do that," said he, "suppose we have two facts: that sup- poses another fact may exist—two men on the earth, one wiser than the other, would logically show that another who is wiser than the wisest may exist. Intelligences exist one above another, so that there is no end to them."

> If Abraham reasoned thus—If Jesus Christ was the Son of God, and John discovered that God the Father of Jesus Christ had a Father, you may suppose that He had a Father also. Where was there ever a son without a father? And where was there ever a father without first being a son? Whenever did a tree or anything spring into existence without a progenitor? And everything comes in this way. Paul says that which is earthly is in the likeness of that which is heavenly, Hence if Jesus had a Father, can we not believe that *He* had a Father also? I despise the idea of being scared to death at such a doctrine, for the Bible is full of it.

have received continue to be carried out by the people at large, the vail will be taken away, so that we can comprehend that Being who is such a mystery to the great portion of the human family.

Jesus was appointed, from the beginning, to die for our redemption, and he suffered an excruciating death on the cross. A person possessing the power of the Gods has that power to sustain him in all his trials and sufferings. He has power and faith to endure unto sweating blood, to bearing thorns, and to being nailed upon a cross, as patiently as did our Saviour. Is this speaking disparagingly of his character? Not in the least. Many of our people have suffered unto death. Could a God do more? He could not. Could he suffer more? Only in proportion to his intelligence, faith, and power, which also proportionally sustain him in his sufferings. Many of the Saints have been pierced with bayonets, riddled with bullets, beaten to death, and slain in various other ways, for their testimony of Jesus. They paid the debt. Jesus fulfilled the obligations he had entered into as the heir of all things pertaining to this earth. He is the King—the Ruler, and the results of the acts of the people he brings forth, and will continue to do so, till he reigns King of nations as he now reigns King of Saints. When he again visits this earth, he will come to thoroughly purge his kingdom from wickedness, and, as ruler of the nations, to dictate and administer to them as the heir to the kingdom; and the Gentiles will be as much mistaken in regard to his second advent as the Jews were in relation to the first.

The eyes of the Gentiles are like the eyes of the fool, wandering to the ends of the earth. They are deceived, blinded, and far from understanding the things of God. All who would understand the things of God must understand them by the Spirit of God. In reflecting upon his providences, it often seems singular that every person cannot understand the things of God; but when you understand the Gospel plan, you will comprehend that it is the most reasonable way of dealing with the human family. You will discern that purity, holiness, justice, perfection, and all that adorns the character of the Deity are contributing to the salvation of man.

Those who acknowledge the hand of God in all things, and abide in his commandments, are the only ones who will sustain the principles of truth and purity. If their influence upon the character is not good and pure, how will they produce that pure feeling, pure faith, and pure godliness which prepare a person to dwell in eternal burnings? Should we not abide in and be influenced by the commandments of God? We should; for, without the spirit of revelation, no man can understand the things of God, nor his dealings and designs in relation to the inhabitants of the earth.

While brother Joseph was referring to the providences of God, I was led to reflect that there is no act, no principle, no power belonging to the Deity that is not purely philosophical. The birth of the Saviour was as natural as are the births of our children; it was the result of natural action. He partook of flesh and blood—was begotten of his Father, as we were of our fathers.

Do you understand yourselves, brethren and sisters? Only to a small degree; and there are as yet but few who can strictly govern themselves. The foundation for all intelligence is placed in man to be developed to produce great and more powerful results than he has ever thought of. You may place all the world's wisdom in one man, and ask him whence he received his intelli-

SUGGESTIONS FOR FAMILY INVOLVEMENT

A Game

Introduce tonight's home evening with the game on the next page. Divide your family into two teams. Cut the game in two along the dotted line. Each team goes off by itself to consult and play the game. One member of a team should read each statement. The team should decide upon the answers and circle whether the statement is true or false. After the answers are marked, the team proceeds on the maze in the direction indicated by the answers. "True" goes left and "false" goes right. Be careful, with one incorrect answer you may arrive at a dead end.

In What Way is Jesus God's Only Son?

Read or tell the following story.

JENNY'S QUESTION

The Markham family had been to Sunday School and was driving home. Brother Markham asked each of his four children what they had learned that day. Each of the children related a story or a teaching that he had learned. When Jenny was asked what she had learned, she replied, "Daddy, I'm confused. The teacher talked about Jesus' being God's only son. I thought all of us were God's children.

Ask, Have you ever wondered about this question? How would you answer Jenny? Discuss this with the family, letting each have a chance to express himself.

Now read to the family how a modern prophet answered Jenny's question.

A MODERN PROPHET'S ANSWER

. . . I want the little folks to hear what I am going to tell you. I am going to tell you a simple truth, yet it is one of the greatest truths and one of the most simple facts ever revealed to the children of men.

You all know that your fathers are indeed your fathers and that your mothers are indeed your mothers—you all know that don't you? You cannot deny it. Now, we are told in scriptures that Jesus Christ is the only begotten Son of God in the flesh. Well, now for the benefit of the older ones, how are children begotten? I answer just as Jesus Christ was begotten of his father. The difference between Jesus Christ and other men is this: Our fathers in the flesh are mortal men, who are subject unto death: but the Father of Jesus Christ in the flesh is the God of Heaven. Therefore Jesus, as he declared, received the

Family Home Evening (1972 edition) p. 125. Copyright © 1972 Corporation of the President of The Church of Jesus Christ of Latter-day Saints.

(Revelation 3:14). In the course of a revelation given through Joseph Smith in May, 1833, the Lord Jesus Christ said as before cited: "And now, verily I say unto you, I was in the beginning with the Father, and am the Firstborn" (D.& C. 93:21). A later verse makes plain the fact that human beings generally were similarly existent in spirit state prior to their embodiment in the flesh: "Ye were also in the beginning with the Father; that which is Spirit, even the Spirit of truth" (verse 23).

There is no impropriety, therefore, in speaking of Jesus Christ as the Elder Brother of the rest of human kind. That He is by spiritual birth Brother to the rest of us is indicated in Hebrews: "Wherefore in all things it behoved him to be made like unto his brethren, that he might be a merciful and faithful high priest in things pertaining to God, to make reconciliation for the sins of the people" (Hebrews 2:17). Let it not be forgotten, however, that He is essentially greater than any and all others, by reason (1) of His seniority as the oldest or firstborn; (2) of His unique status in the flesh as the offspring of a mortal mother and of an immortal, or resurrected and glorified, Father; (3) of His selection and fore-ordination as the one and only Redeemer and Savior of the race; and (4) of His transcendent sinlessness.

Jesus Christ is not the Father of the spirits who have taken or yet shall take bodies upon this earth, for He is one of them. He is The Son, as they are sons and daughters of Elohim. So far as the stages of eternal progression and attainment have been made known through divine revelation, we are to understand that only resurrected and glorified beings can become parents of spirit offspring. Only such exalted souls have reached maturity in the appointed course of eternal life; and the spirits born to them in the eternal worlds will pass in due sequence through the several stages or estates by which the glorified parents have attained exaltation.

THE FIRST PRESIDENCY AND THE COUNCIL
OF THE TWELVE APOSTLES OF THE CHURCH
OF JESUS CHRIST OF LATTER-DAY SAINTS

The Articles of Faith by James E. Talmage, One of the Twelve Apostles of the Church of Jesus Christ of Latter-day Saints, 1988 ed., p. 473. Copyright © 1968 David O. McKay Trustee-in-Trust for The Church of Jesus Christ of Latter-day Saints.

teousness sake? None! They claimed that they did it on account of their wickedness; and if they never have made this acknowledgement, do you think they ever will? No! With a blind and maddened zeal against the Saints, strengthened by the eternal hatred and jealousy of the fallen angels, will they fill the cup of their iniquity and ripen in the glare of their oppression for the judgments of Almighty God.

Are we everywhere spoken against? Is almost every newspaper and journal, with a thousand and one anonymous letter writers, pouring forth their spleen, animadversions, and maledictions upon the Saints in Utah? Do they wish and intend to blow up a storm—a tempest to burst upon our heads with all the fury of the combined elements to sweep us from the face of the earth? Or secretely and under cover, do they intend to rig a purchase to prey upon the peace and happiness of the Saints who have fled from the face of the "serpent," unprotected and unredressed, to this desolate land, to which no other people would come until after we came and killed the snakes, built the bridges, proved the country, raised bread and built houses for them to come to, a land where no other people can or will dwell, should the Mormons leave it!

Why this hatred and ill-will against you? What have you done to provoke it? We have rebuked iniquity; and, in some instances, in rather high places. But the real cause is explained by our Saviour: "Ye are not of the world, but I have chosen you out of the world, therefore the world hate you."

Remember that God not only rules the storm, but visits the secret chambers. He can hush the storm, and say to the winds, "Peace, be still," and catch the fowler in his own snare.

The professed purity of this gene-ration will not allow the institutions of Utah to exist undisturbed, if they can devise any scheme to disturb them. It is true that the people of Utah believe in and practise polygamy. Not because our natural desires lead us into that condition and state of life, but because our God hath commanded it, and wishing to comply with that as well as with all others of His commands, we are as we are. We also wish to be counted Abraham's children, to whom the promises were made, and also with whom the covenants were established; and being told that if we are the children of Abraham, we will do the works of Abraham, we are not a little anxious to do as he did. Among other things that he did, he took more than one wife. In this he was not alone, for this example was copied by most of the ancient worthies and others who succeeded him under the same everlasting covenant. Even the wisest and best men—men after God's own heart, entered the most deeply into this practice. Nor was this practice limited to the days of the Old Testament.

It will be borne in mind that once on a time, there was a marriage in Cana of Galilee; and on a careful reading of that transaction, it will be discovered that no less a person than Jesus Christ was married on that occasion. If he was never married, his intimacy with Mary and Martha, and the other Mary also whom Jesus loved, must have been highly unbecoming and improper to say the best of it.

I will venture to say that if Jesus Christ were now to pass through the most pious countries in Christendom with a train of women, such as used to follow him, fondling about him, combing his hair, anointing him with precious ointment, washing his feet with tears, and wiping them with the hair of their heads and unmarried, or even mar-

and reputation here that it has in London, New York, Boston, Philadelphia, or Washington, then we might be comparatively silent while such vices carried the popular sway. But anything unusual, and of a corrupting character in our midst, excites in us an indignation that often finds vent in maledictions upon the heads of the demons that attempt to introduce it.

If there were none but Latter-day Saints living in Utah, we should have no occasion to speak upon this subject as we do; but being infested by those "*who profess the pure morality of the religion of Jesus*," such as the *Charleston Mercury* endorses and eulogizes, we are constrained to speak in great plainness. I will now leave this subject, knowing that he or she that is righteous will be righteous still; and they who are filthy will be filthy still.

I discover that some of the Eastern papers represent me as a great blasphemer, because I said, in my lecture on Marriage, at our last Conference, that Jesus Christ was married at Cana of Galilee, that Mary, Martha, and others were his wives, and that he begat children.

All that I have to say in reply to that charge is this—they worship a Savior that is too pure and holy to fulfil the commands of his Father. I worship one that is just pure and holy enough " to fulfil all righteousness;" not only the righteous law of baptism, but the still more righteous and important law " to multiply and replenish the earth." Startle not at this! for even the Father himself honored that law by coming down to Mary, without a natural body, and begetting a son; and if Jesus begat children, he only " did that which he had seen his Father do."

But to return to our subject—the fellowship of the world. Unite with them just as far as you require them to unite with you, and upon the same principle. If they are hungry, feed them when in your power. If they are in distress, trouble, or difficulty, relieve them. Take them in when strangers, if they ask you. Be kind unto them and courteous; yet remember that God has given to you His Holy Spirit as a standard, to which the world should come. It is your duty to honor that standard, and to keep it erect. If the world have fellowship and union with you, let it be in the Spirit of the Lord. But if you allow that standard to fall in your own hearts, or to become recumbent, and you slide back into the spirit of the world and unite with them, you have virtually struck your colors to the enemy, and gone over to his side! The salt has lost its savor, and is become powerless to save. It is only fit to be cast out and trodden under foot of men.

If you love and respect the welfare of the world, never allow yourselves to imbibe their spirit, or to become one with them. For if you do, you cannot be a savior, but need one as well as they; for you both stand upon one and the same level. The world hated the Savior before they hated us, and they killed him because he would never unite in heart and spirit with them. They will kill some of us for the same cause. But blessed are the man and the woman that are hated by the world because they will not be one with them. " Do them all the good you can, and as little harm as possible."

In conclusion, the present is an important era, an era in which the nations are becoming angry. They thirst for each other's blood; and who knows but that all nations will, respectively, file off under the heads of Greek and Roman, or " Gog and Magog," to fight the terrible battles spoken of in sacred writ?

Ye Saints of Latter-days, keep your lamps trimmed and burning, that you walk not in darkness. Ye virgins, wise and foolish, awake, for, behold, the

9

The Fruits of Mormonism

A key argument that Mormons use to uphold and defend their faith is, "We are the one true church. You can tell this by our fruits." The wording changes from person to person, but the thought is always the same. The claim is that one of the tests of the truth of Mormonism is its fruits. A Scripture reference is not usually given, but when one is provided it is Matthew 7:17–20, where Jesus said, ". . . Even so every good tree bringeth forth good fruit; but a corrupt tree bringeth forth evil fruit. . . . Wherefore by their fruits ye shall know them."

Eager to display such good fruits, the LDS Church puts a high priority on its public image. Spot TV commercials promote the idea that Mormons live clean, healthy lives serving God together as warm, close-knit families. Young missionary elders in their white shirts and neckties stand out as clean-cut examples of wholesomeness. But is this what Jesus had in mind? Or might such an impressive outward appearance be merely the "sheep's clothing" that Jesus in a previous verse of this passage said "false prophets" would put on when they "come to you" (Matt. 7:15)? What are the real fruits of Mormonism?

In its early days the sect was known for polygamy and violence. In fact, although the practice was officially discontinued[1] over a

1. It should be noted that an April 1991, *New York Times News Service* article, date-lined Colorado City, Arizona, describes the 6000 inhabitants of that town as "fundamentalist Mormons" headed by "Mayor Dan Barlow, who has five wives," and adds, "Most of

hundred years ago, polygamy is still the first thing that comes to many people's minds when Mormons are mentioned. The acts of violence are less well known but indisputably documented. In 1844 a force of several hundred Mormon men sacked and destroyed a newspaper office in Nauvoo, Illinois. And when LDS Church founder Joseph Smith, Jr., died at the hands of a hostile mob a few days later, he was far from a passive victim. Behind bars for his role in the newspaper office raid, he obtained a smuggled pistol and used it to take part in a blazing gun battle against the mob storming the Carthage jail. Smith fired several shots, killing two men and wounding a third, before he himself was shot dead.[2] In 1857 Mormon militia led Indians in an attack on a wagon train, killing 120 non-Mormon men, women, and children in the Mountain Meadows Massacre. In that year's "Utah War" Mormon militia faced off against the United States Army, although actual combat was averted.[3]

These historical facts stand in sharp contrast with the good fruits expected of Christians: ". . . the fruit of the Spirit is love,

---

the people in the area are polygamists or believe in the practice." The article indicates that some 50,000 people in the Rocky Mountain states (usually Utah, Idaho, Montana, Wyoming, Colorado, New Mexico, Arizona, and Nevada) live in polygamous households, and that a local branch of the American Civil Liberties Union is endeavoring to make legal recognition of polygamy "a national cause like gay and lesbian rights." It further quotes Utah Attorney General Paul Van Dam as defending his state's policy against prosecuting polygamists. These fundamentalists are outside the official membership of the LDS Church, which excommunicates polygamists, but their existence in such large numbers in Mormon country is a fruit of Mormonism.

2. Many Mormons will deny this. They should be shown the official account found in their own *History of the Church*, vol. 7, pages 102–3: " . . . Brother Joseph . . . approached the door, and pulling the six-shooter left by Brother Wheelock from his pocket, opened the door slightly, and snapped the pistol six successive times; only three of the barrels, however, were discharged. I afterwards understood that two or three were wounded by these discharges, two of whom, I am informed, died."

3. On October 7, 1857, Brigham Young stirred his Mormon audience with these words: " . . . I know that if our enemies intend to try to come here by way of Emigration Kanyon [sic], we shall be ready to meet them; and if they intend to come round by the Malad, we shall be ready to meet them; and if they undertake to come by Fort Hall, we shall be ready to meet them. . . . let your prayers ascend in behalf of the brethren who are in the mountains. . . . The time has arrived when we have either to be trodden under foot by our enemies and die, or to defend ourselves and our rights. . . . we will not submit to such wicked and unlawful treatment, whether it comes from United States or united hell, for the terms are synonymous as the Government is now conducted. . . . Captain Van Vliet . . . said he, 'The United States, with an overflowing treasury, can send out ten, twenty, or fifty thousand troops.' I replied, 'I do not care anything about that.' . . . They do not know the Captain of the armies of Israel" (*Journal of Discourses* 5:330–31).

joy, peace, longsuffering, gentleness, goodness, faith, meekness, temperance: against such there is no law" (Gal. 5:22). But Mormons have been taught to view these aspects of their early Church history in a different light. They see the early followers of Joseph Smith as misunderstood and persecuted. Besides, times have changed, they quickly point out. Mormons today are respected members of the community and include in their number several congressmen and senators. Current LDS Church President Ezra Taft Benson served in Washington, D.C., as a cabinet member under President Eisenhower. Mormons now enjoy a reputation as moral, upstanding citizens—sober nondrinkers and nonsmokers who abstain even from nerve-jangling coffee and cola beverages.

But what do the facts really show? Although data is not available on LDS Church members *per se,* statistics are available on geographical areas where they make up the bulk of the population, most significantly the State of Utah, which is 77.2 percent Mormon (year-end 1989) according to the *1991–1992 Church Almanac,* published by Deseret News (p. 332). In Luke 13:20–21 Jesus said, "Whereunto shall I liken the kingdom of God? It is like leaven, which a woman took and hid in three measures of meal, till the whole was leavened." So it would seem reasonable that data on Utah, with its high concentration of Mormons, would accurately reflect the fruits of Mormonism, especially when contrasted with data for the United States as a whole, where less than two percent of the population is affiliated with the sect.

Births per 1000 people[4]		
year	Utah	United States
1986	21.9	15.6
1987	21.0	15.7
1988	21.3	15.9

4. In this chart and those to follow, data is compiled from "Utah Vital Statistics, State of Utah, Department of Health, Office of Administration, Bureau of Vital Records and Health Statistics," State of Utah Office of Planning and Budget; "Vital Statistics of the United States, U.S. Department of Health and Human Services"; "Statistical Abstract of the United States, U.S. Department of Commerce, Economic & Statistics Administration, Bureau of the Census"; *Sourcebook of Criminal Justice Statistics* (United States Department of Justice, 1989); and *Kids Count Data Book* (Center for the Study of Social Policy, Washington, D.C., 1992).

Abortions per 1000 live births[5]		
year	Utah	United States
1984	108	422
1985	116	425
1988	139	404

The higher birth rate and lower abortion rate indicate that Utah statistics do indeed mirror Mormon beliefs and practices, as the Church favors large families and frowns on birth control and abortion. Therefore, other statistics for the state that differ from the United States as a whole can reasonably be assumed to reflect the influence of the LDS Church.[6]

Rapes per 100,000 people		
year	Utah	United States
1987	21.7	37.4
1988	24.0	38.0
1989	29.0	38.0

Murders per 100,000 people		
year	Utah	United States
1987	3.3	8.3
1988	2.8	8.4
1989	2.6	8.7

Violent Crimes per 100,000 people		
year	Utah	United States
1987	230	610
1988	243	637
1989	259	663

These tables for rapes, murders, and violent crimes may seem to support the Mormon side of the argument, that is, that good fruits identify them as the true people of God. But all of the facts are not yet in view. A problem begins to surface when data for all crimes in general and for larceny/theft are examined.

5. Comparisons are for years in which Utah statistics are available.
6. For more extensive data see appendix 2.

Total crimes per 100,000 people		
year	Utah	United States
1987	5619	5550
1988	5579	5664
1989	5682	5741

Larceny/Theft per 100,000 people		
year	Utah	United States
1987	4229	3081
1988	4239	3135
1989	4289	3171

Overall crime figures show that total crime in Utah is about the same as the national average. And larceny is significantly higher than the national average. In fact, some have called Utah the fraud or white-collar crime capital of the United States.[7]

But the most disturbing figures of all come into view when attention is directed to data concerning Utah's families.

Divorce per 1000 people		
year	Utah	United States
1986	5.2	4.9
1987	5.3	4.8
1988	4.6	4.8
1989	4.7	4.7
1990[8]	5.2	4.7

Divorces are about as common in Utah as in the rest of the country, or slightly more common, in spite of the network TV ads on strong family life. Reinforcing the relevance of these statistics, the quarterly *Dialogue: A Journal of Mormon Thought* published in its Fall 1992 issue (vol. 25, no. 3) an article titled "Demographics of the Contemporary Mormon Family" by a Brigham Young University sociology teacher. This article cites a higher divorce rate for Mormons than for Catholics, Jews, Lutherans, Methodists, other Protestants of major denominations, and Fundamentalist Christians.

7. *The Darker Side of Virtue: Corruption, Scandal and the Mormon Empire,* by Anson Shupe (Buffalo: Prometheus Books, 1991), p. 45.
8. *Salt Lake Tribune,* July 5, 1992, p. B-1.

Children fare well in Utah according to some published statistics, such as those found in the *Kids Count Data Book* (Washington, D.C.: Center for the Study of Social Policy, 1992), which ranks the state third in the nation. That rating was earned largely because of Utah's low numbers for unwed teenage mothers, children in poverty, infant mortality, and children in single-parent families. But other statistics paint a different picture. For example, as reported in a September 26, 1992, *Salt Lake Tribune* article (p. C-1) the National Education Association ranked Utah schools as lowest in the country on per pupil expenditures, with larger class sizes than any other state.

Deficiencies also show up in statistics that reflect the happiness of parents and children with the emotional quality of life. Thus, although the state's overall murder rate is low, the rate at which children four years old and younger are being killed is at or above the national average:

Homicides 0–4 years of age per 100,000 children in this age group		
year	Utah	United States
1986	3.72	3.37
1987	4.35	3.32
1988	4.52	3.78

Overall suicides in Utah are roughly 10 percent over the national average:

Suicides per 100,000 people		
year[9]	Utah	United States
1980	13.2	11.9
1983	13.1	12.1
1985	13.1	12.3
1986	14.7	12.8
1988	13.6	12.4

Moreover, suicides among children five to fourteen years of age are dramatically high—twice as many such youngsters killing themselves as in other parts of the United States in some recent years. Why such high instances of older children committing suicide in Utah? Apparently there is a problem with the way children are being

9. Years for which Utah statistics are available.

Suicides 5–14 years of age per 100,000 children in this age group		
year	Utah	United States
1986	0.58	.753
1987	1.99	.735
1988	1.69	.701
1989	1.39	(not available)

reared under Mormonism. In fact, a closer look reveals that Utah parents more frequently try to control their children through the use of drugs than parents in other states. Figures released for 1990 by the U.S. Drug Enforcement Administration show that Utah's per capita usage of Ritalin—methylphenidate, a drug used to control hyperactivity in children—was nearly twice (1.8 times) the national average.[10] Yet, even this was a decrease from previous years. The *Salt Lake Tribune* reported on the front page of its November 19, 1991, issue that "Utah's per capita use of Ritalin fell by 43 percent from 1987 to 1990, knocking the state from the No. 1 to the No. 3 spot nationally." Also, the mainly Mormon state consumed even more dramatic quantities of other drugs used for the same purpose, as shown here:

Top States and U.S. Average Rates grams per 100,000 population		
D-Amphetamine Base[11]	Utah	153.836
Trade name: Obetrol	New Mexico	125.979
(Used to control hyperactivity	Washington	124.324
in children)	Wyoming	117.218
	U.S. Average	49.400

(Utah 3.1 times national average, 22% more than 2nd place state)

DL-Methamphetamine[12]	Utah	48.938
Trade name: Desoxyn	Conn.	40.771
(Used to control hyperactivity	Minnesota	28.613
in children)	New Mexico	27.064
	U.S. Average	6.800

(Utah 7.2 times national average, 20% more than 2nd place state)

10. Generic name: Methylphenidate. September 9, 1991, report by the U.S. Drug Enforcement Administration, p. 5.

11. September 9, 1991, report by the U.S. Drug Enforcement Administration, p. 2.

12. September 9, 1991, report by the U.S. Drug Enforcement Administration, p. 3.

As these figures show, Utah consumed Obetrol at a per capita rate of more than three times the national average and Desoxyn more than seven times. True, there are more children per capita in Utah, but that would account for only a small amount of the excess usage, not the very high figures shown here.[13]

We do not enjoy pointing out the problems in the State of Utah. Such problems are not unique to Mormons. "For all have sinned, and come short of the glory of God" (Rom. 3:23). We point out the problems in Utah only because the missionaries of the LDS Church try to hide them. They would have you think that Mormons are as near perfection as can be attained on earth. Time and again we hear, "You can tell we are the one true Church by our fruits." But the facts show that, while the people of Utah have much to be proud of, there are important areas where the good fruits Jesus told us to look for are not evident. Instead, there are bad fruits in the areas of theft, divorce, murder of young children, suicide especially among older children, and very high usage by children of certain behavior-altering prescription drugs. These are symptomatic of people living under pressure rather than of people being led by God's Spirit.

When an outsider gets involved with LDS missionaries or recruiters for another cultic group, a key motivating factor is often his or her discontent with present circumstances. Your loved one may have been hurt or disappointed or neglected at church and may be hoping to find greener pastures in Mormonism. But if the grass looks greener there, it is only an illusion. The facts enumerated above should help to dispel it.

---

13. 36.4 percent of Utah's population is under the age of eighteen, compared to 25.6 percent of the U.S. population that is under the age of eighteen (*Kids Count Data Book*, pp.18, 110).

10

God's "Prophet"

From Joseph Smith onward, each leader of the Church of Jesus Christ of Latter-day Saints has been designated a prophet. Mormons argue from this that theirs must be the true Church, because the Bible says, "And God hath set some in the church, first apostles, secondarily prophets, thirdly teachers, after that miracles, then gifts of healings, helps, governments, diversities of tongues" (1 Cor. 12:28). Mormons use this verse (and others) to claim that they have a church organization the same as existed in the primitive church Jesus Christ established; that is, that the LDS Church constitutes the restoration of the original Christian church. But it is an easy matter for *any* religious sect to assign such titles as "apostle" and "prophet" to positions within their organization, and, in fact, a number of other groups and denominations do the same thing. Moreover, the Mormon Church fails to follow the first-century A.D. pattern accurately. As clearly stated above in 1 Corinthians 12:28, apostles come first and prophets second, but the LDS organization has this reversed, with prophets first and apostles second.

Still, the most important question to invite your loved one to think about is this: Have the Mormon prophets been true prophets, prophets of the true God? The Bible contains a simple test for separating true prophets from false prophets:

But the prophet, which shall presume to speak a word in my name, which I have not commanded him to speak, or that shall speak in the name of other gods, even that prophet shall die. And if thou say in thine heart, How shall we know the word which the LORD hath not spoken? When a prophet speaketh in the name of the LORD, if the thing follow not, nor come to pass, that is the thing which the LORD hath not spoken, but the prophet hath spoken it presumptuously: thou shalt not be afraid of him (Deut. 18:20–22).

Have Joseph Smith, Brigham Young, and their successors as prophets in the LDS Church (1) spoken in the name of other gods or (2) spoken prophecies that failed to come to pass? If either is the case, then the words of Deuteronomy 18:20–22 condemn them as false prophets. What do the facts show?

For evidence that LDS prophets have spoken in the name of gods other than the LORD (Yahweh or Jehovah), please see chapter 8, "Gods and Goddesses." See also *Mormons Answered Verse by Verse,* particularly the discussions of Genesis 1:26, 27; 2:7; Nehemiah 9:6; Daniel 7:9, 13, 22; and 1 Corinthians 8:5.

There are numerous instances of LDS prophets foretelling future events in which the thing prophesied "followed not nor came to pass." One example that any Mormon can find recorded in his own scripture is Joseph Smith's prophecy concerning New Jerusalem:

> [The] city shall be built, beginning at the temple lot, which is appointed by the finger of the Lord, in the western boundaries of the State of Missouri, and dedicated by the hand of Joseph Smith, Jun., and others with whom the Lord was well pleased.
>
> Verily this is the word of the Lord, that the city New Jerusalem shall be built by the gathering of the saints, beginning at this place, even the place of the temple, which temple shall be reared in this generation.
>
> For verily this generation shall not all pass away until an house shall be built unto the Lord . . . ("Revelation given through Joseph Smith the Prophet, at Kirtland, Ohio, September 22 and 23, 1832," Doctrine and Covenants 84:3–5).

Joseph Smith spoke those prophetic words in 1832, over 160 years ago. That generation passed away without any Mormon temple being built in western Missouri, so the prophecy was false.

Mormons may attempt to defend Joseph Smith's prophecy by claiming that he intended the term *this generation* to have a meaning other than the customary one. They will use Mark 13:30 and Matthew 24:34 to support this. But *Joseph Smith—Matthew 1:34* (his version of Matt. 24:34 in the Bible) in the Mormon scripture Pearl of Great Price says: "Verily, I say unto you, this generation, in which these things shall be shown forth, shall not pass away until all I have told you shall be fulfilled." This clearly shows that in Joseph Smith's understanding of the term *this generation* the clock would not start for Jesus' prophecy until the previously prophesied items occurred. But the temple prophecy (Doctrine and Covenants 84:3–5) contained no contingent items that had to occur first. Even Smith's followers who lived within that generation understood him to mean their own lifetime. Thus, nearly forty years later Apostle Orson Pratt indicated that faithful Mormons were still waiting for the prophecy to come to pass:

> I hope this because God promised in the year 1832 that we should, before the generation then living had passed away, return and build up the City of Zion in Jackson county; that we should return and build up the temple of the Most High where we formerly laid the corner stone. He promised us that He would manifest Himself on that temple, that the glory of God should be upon it; and not only upon the temple, but within it, even a cloud by day and a flaming fire by night.
>
> We believe in these promises as much as we believe in any promise ever uttered by the mouth of Jehovah. The Latter-day Saints just as much expect to receive a fulfillment of that promise during the generation that was in existence in 1832 as they expect that the sun will rise and set to-morrow. Why? Because God cannot lie. He will fulfill all His promises. He has spoken, it must come to pass (Orson Pratt, May 5, 1870, *Journal of Discourses*, vol. 13, p. 362).

Apostle Pratt understood Smith to mean "the generation that was in existence in 1832," and he expected to see a fulfillment before that generation passed away. However, in spite of his faith in Joseph Smith, the prophecy proved false. The Mormon Prophet failed the test of Deuteronomy 18:20–22.

Another Mormon defense is the argument that one error does not make Joseph Smith a false prophet. If your loved one raises this objection, answer with a question: How many people does a man have to murder to be called a murderer? Only one. So, how many false prophecies does a prophet have to make to be a false prophet? The answer is obvious.

Nevertheless, lest someone claim that Smith made a single "mistake," another prophecy of his that failed to come to pass should be noted:

> I prophesy in the name of the Lord God of Israel, unless the United States redress the wrongs committed upon the Saints in the state of Missouri and punish the crimes committed by her officers that in a few years the government will be utterly overthrown and wasted, and there will not be so much as a potsherd left, for their wickedness in permitting the murder of men, women and children (Joseph Smith, May 18, 1843, *History of the Church*, vol. 5, p. 394).

The fact that the government of the United States is still standing, of course, makes this, too, a false prophecy.

In still another attempt, Smith prophesied concerning his associate David W. Patten. This "Revelation given through Joseph Smith the Prophet, at Far West, Missouri, April 17, 1838" said:

> Verily thus saith the Lord: It is wisdom in my servant David W. Patten, that he settle up all his business as soon as he possibly can, and make a disposition of his merchandise, that he may perform a mission unto me next spring, in company with others, even twelve including himself, to testify of my name and bear glad tidings unto all the world (Doctrine and Covenants 114:1).

Did Patten perform the prophesied mission in the spring of 1839? No. He died in October, 1838, during a gun battle. "In the pursuit, one of the mob fled from behind a tree, wheeled, and shot Captain Patten, who instantly fell, mortally wounded, having received a large ball in his bowels" (*History of the Church*, vol. 3, p. 171). With Patten dead in 1838, he could not, of course, perform a mission in company with other men in the spring of

1839. So, this is a third prophecy of Joseph Smith that failed to come to pass.[1]

Mormons like to point to their Doctrine and Covenants, section 87, as containing an example of *true* prophecy by Joseph Smith. They see an accurate prediction of the Civil War in this 1832 "revelation and prophecy," stressing these words from verses 1–3: ". . . wars . . . will shortly come to pass, beginning at the rebellion of South Carolina, which will eventually terminate in the death and misery of many souls. . . . For behold, the Southern States shall be divided against the Northern States." However, the political tension between northern and southern states in 1832 was sufficient cause for anyone to speculate on possible armed conflict, even without a supernatural revelation. Moreover, examination of the full text of verses 1–3 shows Smith's words not to fit the Civil War that broke out nearly thirty years later, since he prophesied that the conflict "beginning at this place" would expand to involve Great Britain, "other nations," and then "all nations." Contrary to this prophecy, history shows that the American Civil War ended without becoming an international conflict.

Smith's successor, Brigham Young, also tried his hand at prophesying future events. For example, he foretold that the Civil War would not result in freeing the black slaves.

> Will the present struggle free the slave? No; but they are now wasting away the black race by thousands (Brigham Young, speaking on October 6, 1863, at a General Conference. *Journal of Discourses*, vol. 10, p. 250. See footnote in chapter 8, "Gods and Goddesses.").

History proves this prophecy to be false; events did not follow or come to pass as Brigham Young said they would. Still, he persisted in prophesying.

---

1. A Mormon may claim that death did not prevent David Patten from fulfilling the prophecy, that he did go on a mission as predicted, but that he did it in the spirit world. If this argument is raised, an appropriate answer would be that (a) the prophecy said nothing about the spirit world, but rather that he would "bear glad tidings unto all *the world*," that is, to people living on earth; (b) it said "next spring," whereas Patten's departure in death occurred in the autumn; (c) he was predicted to go in company with others totaling twelve, but that number did not die with him.

Do you think that we shall ever be admitted as a State into the Union without denying the principle of polygamy? If we are not admitted until then, we shall never be admitted (Brigham Young, August 19, 1866, *Journal of Discourses*, vol. 11, p. 269).

With the Mormon Church abandoning the practice of polygamy in 1890, followed by Utah's almost immediate admission to the Union as a state, this prophecy, too, proved false.

Numerous other examples could be furnished, but those listed above are sufficient to discredit the claim that Mormon "prophets" actually speak for God.

What about the Book of Mormon itself? Unlike the Bible, it is not a prophetic book for the most part but purports to be a history of peoples inhabiting the Americas in ancient times. However, it does contain a brief prophecy in which, allegedly, "Joseph in Egypt . . . prophesied of Joseph Smith, the latter-day seer" (2 Nephi 3, chapter heading). Yet, that prophecy proved false, because it said: "And thus prophesied Joseph, saying: Behold, that seer will the Lord bless; and they that seek to destroy him shall be confounded" (2 Nephi 3:14). Instead, what actually came to pass was that those who sought to destroy Joseph Smith succeeded, shooting and killing him on June 27, 1844.

After examining the evidence presented here, review with your loved one the test outlined at Deuteronomy 18:20–22. Ask, Do the Mormon prophets fall into the category of true prophets or false prophets? Why? Explain that the matter is serious because God has said that prophets who lead people to "go after other gods" should "be put to death" (Deut. 13:1–5).

You may wish, however, to show your friend that the Mormon prophets actually do have a part in *fulfilling* Bible prophecy. The Scripture verse they help fulfill is Matthew 24:11, where Jesus foretold that "many false prophets shall rise, and shall deceive many." Encourage your loved one not to be among the many who are deceived.

3 Which city shall be *built, beginning at the *temple lot, which is appointed by the finger of the Lord, in the western boundaries of the State of Missouri, and *dedicated by the hand of Joseph Smith, Jun., and others with whom the Lord was well pleased.

4 Verily this is the word of the Lord, that the city *New Jerusalem shall be built by the gathering of the saints, beginning at this place, even the place of the temple, which *temple shall be *reared in this *generation.

5 For verily this generation shall not all *pass away until an *house shall be built unto the Lord, and a *cloud shall rest upon it, which cloud shall be even the *glory of the Lord, which shall fill the house.

6*And the *sons of Moses, according to the Holy Priesthood which he received under the *hand of his father-in-law, *Jethro;

11 And Gad under the hand of Esaias;

12 And Esaias received it under the hand of God.

13 *Esaias also lived in the days of Abraham, and was blessed of him—

14 Which *Abraham received the priesthood from *Melchizedek, who received it through the lineage of his fathers, even till *Noah;

15 And from Noah till *Enoch, through the lineage of their fathers;

16 And from Enoch to *Abel, who was slain by the *conspiracy of his brother, who *received the priesthood by the commandments of God, by the hand of his father *Adam, who was the first man—

17 Which *priesthood *continueth in the church of God in all generations, and is without *beginning of days or end of years.

18 And the Lord confirmed a *priesthood also upon *Aaron and

Doctrine and Covenants 84:3-5. Copyright © 1981 Corporation of the President of The Church of Jesus Christ of Latter-day Saints.

for aught I know. Suffice it to say, we have over a hundred towns, cities and villages built up in the various portions of this great Basin, this desert country. We have beautified our inheritances; we have planted fruit trees in abundance and ornamental shade trees, so as to make our residences cheering and beautiful in the midst of a desert. God has been with us from the time that we came to this land, and I hope that the days of our tribulation are past. I hope this, because God promised in the year 1832 that we should, before the generation then living had passed away, return and build up the City of Zion in Jackson County; that we should return and build up the temple of the Most High where we formerly laid the corner stone. He promised us that He would manifest Himself on that temple, that the glory of God should be upon it; and not only upon the temple, but within it, even a cloud by day and a flaming fire by night.

We believe in these promises as much as we believe in any promise ever uttered by the mouth of Jehovah. The Latter-day Saints just as much expect to receive a fulfilment of that promise during the generation that was in existence in 1832 as they expect that the sun will rise and set to-morrow. Why? Because God cannot lie. He will fulfil all His promises. He has spoken, it must come to pass. This is our faith. It will depend upon the conduct of the Latter-day Saints whether we suffer more tribulation. We may suffer tribulation although we are righteous in every respect, though there were no sin found in the midst of the people. Why? Because the wicked always did persecute the righteous, they always did hate the principles and plan of salvation; still we have greater claim upon the arm of Jehovah for protection and assistance when we keep His commandments and love and serve Him.

Did you ever hear of the Elders of this Church getting up like the sectarian world and speaking about the love of God dwelling in their bosoms, and saying how much they loved Jesus, and at the same time transgressing his laws? No, we have no right to make any such declaration as this; hence we show to the heavens that we are determined to do the will of God. Then we may say that we love God; then we can say that we love His ways, and His Priesthood, and His Church, and His kingdom, and His Gospel which He has sent forth by His angels in the latter day.

I feel truly grateful to the Most High God that such a great improvement has been made among the Latter-day Saints in these mountains. I think I am able to judge. I have been with this people from my youth up. Forty years have almost expired since I was baptized into this Church and kingdom. I have known the former history of the Saints; and I know and understand, in some measure, their present condition, and I can contrast the two, and I see a decided improvement. Is there more union amongst them? Yes; far more than there was in the lifetime of Joseph; and all that the great mass of the people want is to know what God requires, and, with one heart and mind, they will do it. If God requires them to be baptized for their dead, as far as they can search and find out their ancestors' names, they will do it with all their hearts and souls. If He requires them to receive the sacred ordinance of the endowments, by which they may attain to greater blessings and glory in His presence, they will go to with one heart and mind to receive those ordinances. If God requires His people to take a plurality of depreciation of the conduct of Governor Boggs and the authorities of Missouri, who had taken part in the extermination, and said that any people that would do as the mobs of Missouri had done ought to be brought to judgment: they ought to be punished.

President Smith, in concluding his remarks, said that if the government, which received into its coffers the money of citizens for its public lands, while its officials are rolling in luxury at the expense of its public treasury, cannot protect such citizens in their lives and property, it is an old granny anyhow; and I prophesy in the name of the Lord God of Israel, unless the United States redress the wrongs committed upon the Saints in the state of Missouri and punish the crimes committed by her officers that in a few years the government will be utterly overthrown and wasted, and there will not be so much as a potsherd left, for their wickedness in permitting the murder of men, women and children, and the wholesale plunder and extermination of thousands of her citizens to go unpunished, thereby perpetrating a foul and corroding blot upon the fair fame of this great republic, the very thought of which would have caused the high-minded and patriotic framers of the Constitution of the United States to hide their faces with shame. Judge, you will aspire to the presidency of the United States; and if ever you turn your hand against me or the Latter-day Saints, you will feel the weight of the hand of Almighty upon you; and you will live to see and know that I have testified the truth to you; for the conversation of this day will stick to you through life.

He [Judge Douglas] appeared very friendly, and acknowledged the truth and propriety of President Smith's remarks.*

Joseph Smith, May 18, 1843, *History of the Church,* vol. 5, p. 394. Copyright © 1978 Deseret Book Company.

SECTION 114

Revelation given through Joseph Smith the Prophet, at Far West, Missouri, April 17, 1838. HC 3: 23.

1–2, Church positions held by those who are not faithful shall be given to others.

VERILY thus saith the Lord: It is wisdom in my servant David W. Patten, that he settle up all his business as soon as he possibly can, and make a disposition of his merchandise, that he may "perform a mission unto me next spring, in company with others, even twelve including himself, to testify of my name and bear glad tidings unto all the world.

2 For verily thus saith the Lord, that inasmuch as there are those among you who "deny my name, others shall be "planted in their "stead and receive their "bishopric. Amen.

Doctrine and Covenants 114:1. Copyright © 1981 Corporation of the President of The Church of Jesus Christ of Latter-day Saints.

the ford and such places as they could get a chance. In the pursuit, one of the mob fled from behind a tree, wheeled, and shot Captain Patten, who instantly fell, mortally wounded, having received a large ball in his bowels.

The ground was soon cleared, and the brethren gathered up a wagon or two, and making beds therein of tents, etc, took their wounded and retreated towards Far West.   Three brethren were

List of Casualties. Death

History of the Church, October, 1838, vol. 3, p. 171. Copyright © 1978 Deseret Book Company.

SECTION 87

Revelation and prophecy on war, given through Joseph Smith the Prophet, December 25, 1832. HC 1: 301–302. This section was received at a time when the brethren were reflecting and reasoning upon African slavery on the American continent and the slavery of the children of men throughout the world.

1–4, War foretold between the Northern States and the Southern States; 5–8, Great calamities shall fall upon all the inhabitants of the earth.

VERILY, thus saith the Lord concerning the "wars that will *b*shortly come to pass, beginning at the rebellion of *c*South Carolina, which will eventually terminate in the death and misery of many souls;

2 And the "time will come that *b*war will be poured out upon all nations, beginning at this place.

3 For behold, the Southern States shall be divided against the Northern States, and the Southern States will call on other nations, even the nation of Great Britain, as it is called, and they shall also call upon other nations, in order to defend themselves against other nations; and then "war shall be poured out upon all nations.

4 And it shall come to pass, after many days, "slaves shall rise up against their masters, who shall be marshaled and disciplined for war.

5 And it shall come to pass also that the "remnants who are left of the land will marshal themselves, and shall become exceedingly angry, and shall vex the Gentiles with a sore vexation.

6 And thus, with the "sword and by bloodshed the inhabitants of the earth shall *b*mourn; and with *c*famine, and plague, and earthquake, and the thunder of heaven, and the fierce and vivid lightning also, shall the inhabitants of the earth be made to feel the wrath, and indignation, and *d*chastening *e*hand of an Almighty God, until the consumption decreed hath made a full *f*end of all *g*nations;

7 That the cry of the saints, and of the "blood of the saints, shall cease to come up into the ears of the Lord of *b*Sabaoth, from the earth, to be avenged of their enemies.

8 Wherefore, "stand ye in holy places, and be not moved, until the day of the Lord come; for behold, it cometh *b*quickly, saith the Lord. Amen.

Joseph Smith, December 25, 1832, Doctrine and Covenants 87:1–3. Copyright ©1981 Corporation of the President of The Church of Jesus Christ of Latter-day Saints.

What is the cause of all this waste of life and treasure ? To tell it in a plain, truthful way, one portion of the country wish to raise their negroes or black slaves, and the other portion wish to free them, and, apparently, to almost worship them. Well, raise and worship them, who cares ? I should never fight one moment about it, for the cause of human improvement is not in the least advanced by the dreadful war which now convulses our unhappy country.

Ham will continue to be the servant of servants, as the Lord has decreed, until the curse is removed. Will the present struggle free the slave ? No; but they are now wasting away the black race by thousands. Many of the blacks are treated worse than we treat our dumb brutes ; and men will be called to judgment for the way they have treated the negro, and they will receive the condemnation of a guilty conscience, by the just Judge whose attributes are justice and truth.

Treat the slaves kindly and let them live, for Ham must be the servant of servants until the curse is removed. Can you destroy the decrees of the Almighty ? You cannot. Yet our Christian brethren think that they are going to overthrow the sentence of the Almighty upon the seed of Ham. They cannot do that, though they may kill them by thousands and tens of thousands.

According to accounts, in all probability not less than one million men, from twenty to forty years of age, have gone to the silent grave in this useless war, in a little over two years, and all to gratify the caprice of a few,—I do not think I have a suitable name for them, shall we call them abolitionists; slaveholders, religious bigots, or political aspirants ? Call them what you will, they are wasting away each other, and it seems as though they will not be satisfied until they have brought universal destruction and desolation upon the whole country. It appears as though they would destroy every person ; perhaps they will, but I think they will not.

God rules. Do you know it ? It is the kingdom of God or nothing for the Latter-day Saints.

Do you know that it is the eleventh hour of the reign of Satan on the earth ? Jesus is coming to reign, and all you who fear and tremble because of your enemies, cease to fear them, and learn to fear to offend God, fear to trangress his laws, fear to do any evil to your brother, or to any being upon the earth, and do not fear Satan and his power, nor those who have only power to slay the body, for God will preserve his people.

We are constantly gathering new clay into the mill. How many of the new comers I have heard say, " Oh that I had been with you when you had your trials." We have promised them all the trials that are necessary, if they would be patient.

Are you going to be patient and trust in God, and receive every trial with thanksgiving, acknowledging the hand of the Lord in it ? You will have all the trial you can bear. The least thing tries some people. Brother Heber and myself going to the island in Great Salt Lake, a week ago last Friday, created numerous surmisings and misgivings with some. I have thought that it might, perhaps, be well to notify you regularly, through the *Deseret News*, of my outgoings and in-comings ; and I may as well now notify you that it is my intention to visit Sanpete, and, perhaps, our southern settlements this fall. If I should do so, I hope that my brethren and sisters will feel satisfied, for I shall go, come, stay and act as I feel dictated by the Spirit of God God being my helper, asking no odds of any person.—Amen.

blessings which Abraham obtained, you will be polygamists at least in your faith, or you will come short of enjoying the salvation and the glory which Abraham has obtained. This is as true as that God lives. You who wish that there were no such thing in existence, if you have in your hearts to say: "We will pass along in the Church without obeying or submitting to it in our faith or believing this order, because, for aught that we know, this community may be broken up yet, and we may have lucrative offices offered to us; we will not, therefore, be polygamists lest we should fail in obtaining some earthly honor, character and office, etc,"— the man that has that in his heart, and will continue to persist in pursuing that policy, will come short of dwelling in the presence of the Father and the Son, in celestial glory. The only men who become Gods, even the Sons of God, are those who enter into polygamy. Others attain unto a glory and may even be permitted to come into the presence of the Father and the Son; but they cannot reign as kings in glory, because they had blessings offered unto them, and they refused to accept them.

The Lord gave a revelation through Joseph Smith, His servant; and we have believed and practiced it. Now, then, it is said that this must be done away before we are permitted to receive our place as a State in the Union. It may be, or it may not be. One of the twin relics—slavery— they say, is abolished. I do not, however, wish to speak about this; but if slavery and oppression and iron-handed cruelty are not more felt by the blacks to-day than before, I am glad of it. My heart is pained for that unfortunate race of men. One twin relic having been strangled, the other, they say, must next be destroyed. It is they and God for it,

and you will all find that out. It is not Brigham Young, Heber C. Kimball and Daniel H. Wells and the Elders of Israel they are fighting against; but it is the Lord Almighty. What is the Lord going to do? He is going to do just as he pleases, and the world cannot help themselves.

I heard the revelation on polygamy, and I believed it with all my heart, and I know it is from God— I know that he revealed it from heaven; I know that it is true, and understand the bearings of it and why it is. "Do you think that we shall ever be admitted as a State into the Union without denying the principle of polygamy?" If we are not admitted until then, we shall never be admitted. These things will be just as the Lord will. Let us live to take just what he sends to us, and when our enemies rise up against us, we will meet them as we can, and exercise faith and pray for wisdom and power more than they have, and contend continually for the right. Go along, my children, saith the Lord, do all you can, and remember that your blessings come through your faith. Be faithful and cut the corners of your enemies where you can—get the advantage of them by faith and good works, take care of yourselves, and they will destroy themselves. Be what you should be, live as you should, and all will be well.

Who knows but the time will come when the inquiry will be made in Washington, by the President, by the Congressmen: "Are things any worse in Utah than in Washington: than they are in New York? or in any State of the Union? are they more unvirtuous, are they more disloyal to the Government? But then there is polygamy." That has nothing in the least to do with our being loyal or disloyal, one way or the other. But is not the practice of

11

"Restored," Then Changed Again

Brigham Young declared in 1870, "I have never yet preached a sermon and sent it out to the children of men, that they may not call Scripture" *(Journal of Discourses* 13:95). Later that same year he repeated that claim and added concerning his sermons that "when they are copied and approved by me they are as good Scripture as is couched in this Bible" *(Journal of Discourses* 13:264). In 1873 he challenged his audience to "bring up the first idea, the first sentence that I have delivered to the people as counsel that is wrong. I really wish they would do it; but they cannot do it, for the simple reason that I have never given counsel that is wrong; this is the reason" *(Journal of Discourses* 16:161). Similarly, Joseph Smith spoke of "the power of truth in the doctrines which I have been an instrument in the hands of God of presenting" and challenged his enemies to "strike a blow at the doctrine" he taught, asserting, "They cannot do it: it is truth, and I defy all men to upset it" (March 24, 1844, *History of the Church,* vol. 6, p. 273). On another occasion Smith added, "When did I ever teach anything wrong from this stand? . . . I never told you I was perfect; but there is no error in the revelations which I have taught" (May 2, 1844, *Teachings of the Prophet Joseph Smith,* p. 368).

Yet, if Brigham Young and Joseph Smith, Jr., taught the truth, why have so many of their teachings been contradicted, changed, or abandoned? The following examples of such changes may help a Mormon to begin questioning the validity of what the LDS Church presents as truth today.

Concerning deacons, Brigham Young taught in 1854 that a bishop should say, "I dare not even call a man to be a Deacon, to assist me in my calling, unless he has a family. It is not the business of an ignorant young man . . . but select a man who has got a family to be a Deacon, whose wife can go with him, and assist him in administering to the needy in the ward. . . . the view I take of the matter is not to be disputed or disproved by Scripture or reason" (*Journal of Discourses* 2:89). Today, however, the official practice is, "When a boy has been baptized and confirmed a member of the Church and is worthy, he may be ordained to the office of deacon when he is twelve years old" (*Gospel Principles*, 1986 ed., p. 81).

Mormons have also been taught to change their minds on the way children rise from the dead. Speaking at an official Church conference held near the Temple in Nauvoo, Illinois, on April 6, 1844, President Joseph Smith taught:

> . . . as the child dies, so shall it rise from the dead, and be for ever living in the learning of God. It will never grow: it will still be the child, in the same precise form as it appeared before it died out of its mother's arms, but possessing all the intelligence of a God (*Journal of Discourses* 6:10).

Today, however, the official textbook *Gospel Principles* teaches the opposite:

> All spirits are in adult form. They were adults before their mortal existence, and they are in adult form after death, even if they die as infants or children . . . (1986 ed., p. 278).

Ask your loved one which teaching he believes, the official pronouncement of Joseph Smith, or the modern textbook. Ask him why he thinks Mormons teach differently today.

Some might attempt to dismiss the above with the objection that these are not major, significant teachings that have been changed. In that case, turn the attention of your loved one to what has been taught about the very person and nature of God. Joseph Smith said, "It is the first principle of the Gospel to know for a certainty the character of God" (at General Conference, April 6, 1844, *Journal of Discourses* 6:3; *Teachings of the Prophet Joseph Smith*, p. 345; and *History of the Church*, vol. 6, p. 305). Smith also stated that one of "three things . . . necessary, in order that any rational and intelligent being may exercise faith in God unto life and salvation" is "A *correct* idea of his character, perfections and attributes" (emphasis in the original, Doctrine and Covenants, 1835 ed., "Lecture Third of Faith," p. 36, vv. 2–4). Moreover, Brigham Young said, "It is one of the first principles of the doctrine of salvation to become acquainted with our Father and our God" (*Journal of Discourses* 4:215). Brigham Young then quoted from John 17:3 about knowing the only true God and Jesus whom he sent, and commented, ". . . this is as much as to say that *no man* can enjoy or be prepared for eternal life *without* that knowledge" *(emphasis added)*. With this in mind, go on to discuss with your loved one what was taught about the nature of God. The original 1835 edition of Doctrine and Covenants taught this in "Lecture Fifth of Faith,"[1] section V, verse 2, pages 52–53:

> There are two personages who constitute the great, matchless, governing and supreme power over all things—by whom all things were created and made, that are created and made, whether visible or invisible: whether in heaven, on earth, or in the earth, under the earth, or throughout the immensity of space—They are the Father and the Son: The Father being a personage of spirit,[2] glory and power: possessing all perfection and fulness: The Son, who was in the bosom of the Father, a personage of tabernacle, made, or fashioned like unto a man, or being in the form and likeness of man, or, rather, man was formed after his likeness, and in his image.

The same verse continues to add:

> And he being the only begotten of the Father, full of grace and truth, and having overcome, received a fulness of the glory of the Father— possessing the same mind with the Father, which mind is the Holy

---

1. *The Lectures on Faith* were the doctrine part of the original Doctrine and Covenants. They were quietly removed in 1921 without the prior approval of the membership, that is without the "common consent" required for such changes according to Doctrine and Covenants 26:2 and 28:13.

2. This is also found in the Book of Mormon at Alma 31:15, 18:2–5, 26–28 and Mosiah 15:1–5, in Doctrine and Covenants 93:21–23, and in the Bible at John 4:24.

Spirit, that bears record of the Father and the Son, and these three are one, or in other words, these three constitute the great, matchless, governing and supreme power over all things.

And on page 55 of this same reference we have the following:

Q. How many personages are there in the Godhead?
A. Two: the Father and the Son. [§5. ¶1.]
Q. How do you prove that there are two personages in the Godhead?
A. By the Scriptures.

Note that the 1835 edition of Doctrine and Covenants here declares the Father to be "a personage of spirit," not "a personage of tabernacle" (fleshly body) as the Son is said to be, and that there are only two personages. Today's Doctrine and Covenants no longer contains this discussion of deity, as it was removed in 1921; instead, section 130:22 says:

The Father has a body of flesh and bones as tangible as man's; the Son also; but the Holy Ghost has not a body of flesh and bones, but is a personage of Spirit.

So, over the course of its history the LDS Church has changed its teaching on whether or not God the Father has a "tabernacle" (body). Note, too, that the Holy Ghost has been changed from the mind shared by the "two personages," the Father and the Son, in the 1835 scripture, to a third "personage" in today's. If Joseph Smith and Brigham Young taught mistaken ideas about this important "first principle," what other errors might they have taught? Such uncertainty as to the person and nature of God surely should call into question whether the LDS Church has got it right yet.

When the Mormon Church was founded on April 6, 1830, it was officially named the Church of Christ. Later, at a conference of elders on May 3, 1834, with Joseph Smith, Jr., as moderator, the name was changed to The Church of the Latter Day Saints by unanimous vote (The Evening and Morning Star, May 1834, vol. 2, no. 20, p. 160; also, History of the Church 2:62–63). Why, then, did Mormon Apostle Bruce McConkie claim in his book Mormon

Doctrine, "One or more of the names of Christ has always been in the formal name of the Church," when the name of Christ was removed in 1834 (1979 ed., p. 136)? Again, on April 26, 1838, it was renamed The Church of Jesus Christ of Latter-day Saints, its present designation. If Joseph Smith was truly speaking for God (the Book of Mormon in 3 Nephi 27:6–8 says, "therefore ye shall call the church in my name. . . . And how be it my church save it be called in my name?"), why was there such confusion about the name of the church during its first decade?

Back-and-forth changes in the matter of polygamy should also be of concern to sincere believers. The Book of Mormon, first published in 1830, condemns polygamy throughout; see, for example, Jacob 2:24, Mosiah 11:2, and Ether 10:5, all of which denounce kings for having "many wives and concubines."[3] The LDS Church indicates, however, that Joseph Smith, Jr., knew "the doctrines and principles" of plural marriage "since 1831," the year following publication of the Book of Mormon (Doctrine and Covenants, 1990 printing, section 132 introduction). The 1835 edition of Doctrine and Covenants included section 101, verse 4, which said, "Inasmuch as this church of Christ has been reproached with the crime of fornication, and polygamy: we declare that we believe, that one man should have one wife; and one woman, but one husband." This was included in all editions until 1876, when it was quietly removed. However, Mormons and their leaders were practicing polygamy throughout that entire period. The 1876 edition of Doctrine and Covenants added section 132, establishing polygamy as an "everlasting covenant" such that "if ye abide not that covenant, then are ye damned; for no one can reject this covenant and be permitted to enter into my glory" (132:4). And this new section was approved by membership vote as a part of Mormon canonized scripture in 1880 (*Ensign*, December 1984, pp. 38–39). But just ten years later, in 1890, the Manifesto was

---

3. A contradiction should be noted between Jacob 2:24, which says, "Behold, David and Solomon truly had many wives and concubines, *which thing was abominable before me, saith the Lord*," and Doctrine and Covenants 132:38–39, which says, "David also received many wives and concubines, and also Solomon and Moses my servants, as also many others of my servants, from the beginning of creation until this time; and in nothing did they sin save in those things which they received not of me. David's wives and concubines were given unto him of me . . . and in none of these things did he sin against me save in the case of Uriah and his wife" *(emphasis added).*

issued officially ending the practice of polygamy by LDS Church members. Still, Doctrine and Covenants 132 establishing the practice as an "everlasting covenant" remains part of Mormon scripture. Such a history of back-and-forth changes, with public statements contradicting private practice much of the time, is confusing to say the least. Ask your Mormon friend if the persons implementing these changes could have been acting as a mouthpiece for the God who is "not the author of confusion" (1 Cor. 14:33).

is no matter if the whole world is against us, God is for us. Could not they kill you? Yes, if it be the Lord's will. If it be the will of the Lord for the people to live, they will live. If it had been the will of the Lord that Joseph and Hyrum should have lived, they would have lived. It was necessary for Joseph to seal his testimony with his blood. Had he been destined to live he would have lived. The Lord suffered his death to bring justice on the nation. The debt is contracted and they have it to pay. The nations of the earth are in the Lord's hands; and if we serve Him we shall reap the reward of so doing. If we neglect to obey His laws and ordinances, we shall have to suffer the consequences.

Well, brethren and sisters, try and be Saints. I will try; I have tried many years to live according to the law which the Lord reveals unto me. I know just as well what to teach this people and just what to say to them and what to do in order to bring them into the celestial kingdom, as I know the road to my office. It is just as plain and easy. The Lord is in our midst. He teaches the people continually. I have never yet preached a sermon and sent it out to the children of men, that they may not call Scripture. Let me have the privilege of correcting a sermon, and it is as good Scripture as they deserve. The people have the oracles of God continually. In the days of Joseph, revelation was given and written, and the people were driven from city to city and place to place, until we were led into these mountains. Let this go to the people with "Thus saith the Lord," and if they do not obey it, you will see the chastening hand of the Lord upon them. But if they are plead with, and led along like children, we may come to understand the will of the Lord and He may preserve us as we desire.

Let us, then, you and me and all who profess to be Latter-day Saints, try to be Saints indeed. God bless you, Amen.

DISCOURSE BY ELDER GEORGE Q. CANNON,

DELIVERED IN THE NEW TABERNACLE, SALT LAKE CITY, APRIL 6, 1869.

(Reported by David W. Evans.)

THE ORDER OF ENOCH—SOCIALISTIC EXPERIMENTS—THE SOCIAL PROBLEM.

I look upon this Conference as one of the most important, in many respects, that we have ever had the privilege of participating in, for, to my view, there are more interesting and important events connected with the work of God at the present time than have ever been developed before in our history. We are undergoing a great change, a great revolution is it? Very little. There may be some minds which could grasp some things pertaining to it, but others could not. The spirit of revelation can reveal these things to the people, but unless they live so as to have the revelations of the Lord Jesus Christ, they will remain a mystery, for there is a vail before the minds of the people, and they cannot be understood. Some of these principles have been taught to the Latter-day Saints, but who can understand them?

Brother Orson Hyde referred to a few who complained about not getting revelations. I will make a statement here that has been brought against me as a crime, perhaps, or as a fault in my life. Not here, I do not allude to anything of the kind in this place, but in the councils of the nations—that Brigham Young has said "when he sends forth his discourses to the world they may call them Scripture." I say now, when they are copied and approved by me they are as good Scripture as is couched in this Bible, and if you want to read revelation read the sayings of him who knows the mind of God, without any special command to one man to go here, and to another to go yonder, or to do this or that, or to go and settle here or there. In the early days of the Church, if a man was going to sell a farm he must have a revelation—Joseph must receive and give a revelation. Many men would not do one thing until God had given them a revelation through the prophet. It must be: "Thus saith the Lord, sell your farm, devote such a portion of your means to education, or printing, or for distributing knowledge to the world. Devote such a portion of your means to do this, and such a portion to do that." I have known a good many men in the early days of the Church who had property, that must have revelation to know

what disposition to make of their substance; but who, when they received it, were sure not to strictly obey it. What did revelation do for such persons? Nothing but seal their condemnation. Why do the people want revelations to damn themselves?

Give the mind of the Lord to this people here in this Conference, would they observe it? There is a few who would like to; but take some of those who are called Latter-day Saints, would they follow it if it were given them? I know they would not, still the Lord is merciful and forbearing and He bears with His people. He has borne with and blest us, to see if we would walk in the knowledge of the truth and yield strict obedience to His requirements.

Poverty, persecution and oppression we have endured; many of us have suffered the loss of all things in a worldly point of view. Give us prosperity and see if we would bear it, and be willing to serve God. See if we would be as willing to sacrifice millions as we were to sacrifice what we had when in comparative poverty. Men of property, as a general thing, would not be. We know this, God knows it, and He has to treat us as unruly, disobedient, slow to think and slow to act—as a set of children.

It has been said, time and time again, that if the people would live worthy of the great things God has in store for them, they are ready to come forth for their salvation and edification; but until we improve upon little things and hearken to the voice of the Lord in our first duties, He is not going to bestow the great mysteries of the invisible worlds upon us. We know too much already unless we do better. You may think I am complaining; well, I am just a trifle. I see the Latter-day Saints here and there going to destruction, and pass it over; but this is foolishness. There is not a particle of good sense about it; no light, no intelligence, nothing that is ennobling, elevating, cheering, comforting, consoling, that produces friends, or anything of this kind. I call it foolism; I do it this time, consequently we will not talk anything about apostacy.

When people receive this Gospel, what do they sacrifice? Why, death for life. This is what they give: darkness for light, error for truth, doubt and unbelief for knowledge and the certainty of the things of God, consequently I consider it to be the biggest piece of foolism that can be hatched up, imagined or entertained, or followed out by any human being, to leave this Gospel for what they will receive in exchange. So much for apostacy.

Now a few words, my brethren and sisters, with regard to our position. There are many in this Church who have been with it a long time. This Church has been traveling for many years. The time that this Church has been traveling exceeds the time of the children of Israel in the wilderness.

[At this point the water for the Sacrament was blessed.]

I will give you a word of counsel here with regard to consecrating the bread and the water, which I want the Saints to remember. When you [addressing the Bishops and Elders] administer the Sacrament, take this book [the Book of Doctrine and Covenants] and read this prayer. Take the opportunity to read this prayer until you can remember it. You cannot get up anything that is better, and not even equal to it; and when you read it, read it so that the people can hear you. This is what I wish of you; it is what is right, and that which the Spirit will manifest to you if you inquire; and if you

No. 11.

cannot commit this prayer to memory, the one that is given by revelation expressly for consecrating the bread and the wine, or water, if the latter be used, take the book and read until you can remember. If I were to come here next Sabbath, and see you breaking bread, would this, that I am now mentioning, be thought of? The people have various ideas with regard to this prayer. They sometimes cannot hear six feet from the one who is praying, and in whose prayer, perhaps, there are not three words of the prayer that is in this book, that the Lord tells us that we should use. This is pretty hard on the Elders, is it not? If they could remember one thousandth part of that which they have heard, it would have sanctified them years and years ago; but it goes in at one ear and out at the other—it is like the weaver's shuttle passing through the web.

Now I am going to tell you some more things, and how long will you remember them? Until you get home? Perhaps there are a few who will remember a few words of counsel that I shall give to you. I am here to give this people, called Latter-day Saints, counsel to direct them in the path of life. I am here to answer; I shall be on hand to answer when I am called upon, for all the counsel and for all the instruction that I have given to this people. If there is an Elder here, or any member of this Church, called the Church of Jesus Christ of Latter-day Saints, who can bring up the first idea, the first sentence that I have delivered to the people as counsel that is wrong, I really wish they would do it; but they cannot do it, for the simple reason that I have never given counsel that is wrong; this is the reason. This people, called Latter-day Saints, have been laboring now over forty years. Forty-three years last April,

Vol. XVI.

Brigham Young, August 31, 1873, *Journal of Discourses* 16:161.

but that he can officiate in his office, and magnify it to acceptance.

The office of a Bishop is in his ward; and when he finds a man who is doing a good business as a farmer or a tradesman, and who has plenty around him, and is faithfully paying his tithing, he has no business there only to receive the tithing that man has to pay for the benefit of the kingdom of God; his business is more particularly in the houses of widows and orphans, and he is called to administer to them in righteousness, like a father.

Paul, knowing by observation and his own experience the temptations that were continually thrown before the Elders, gave instructions paramount to this—Before you ordain a person to be a Bishop, to take the charge of a Branch in any one district or place, see that he has a *wife* to begin with; he did not say, "*but one* wife;" it does not read so; but he must have *one* to begin with, in order that he may not be continually drawn into temptation while he is in the line of his duty, visiting the houses of widows and orphans, the poor, the afflicted, and the sick in his ward. He is to converse with families, sometimes upon family matters, and care for them, but if he has no wife, he is not so capable of taking care of a family as he otherwise would be, and perhaps he is not capable of taking care of himself. Now select a young man who has preserved himself in purity and holiness, one who has carried himself circumspectly before the people, and before God: it would not do to ordain him to the office of a Bishop, for he may be drawn into temptation, and he lacks experience in family matters; but take a man who has one wife at least, a man of experience, like thousands of our Elders, men of strength of mind, who have determination in them to preserve themselves pure under all circumstances, at all times, and in all places in their wards. Now, Timothy, select such a man to be a Bishop.

A Bishop in his calling and duty is with the Church all the time; he is not called to travel abroad to preach, but is at home; he is not abroad in the world, but is with the Saints.

When you have got your Bishop, he needs assistants, and he ordains Counsellors, Priests, Teachers, and Deacons, and calls them to help him; and he wishes men of his own heart and hand to do this. Says he, "I dare not even call a man to be a Deacon, to assist me in my calling, unless he has a family." It is not the business of an ignorant young man, of no experience in family matters, to inquire into the circumstances of families, and know the wants of every person. Some may want medicine and nourishment, and to be looked after, and it is not the business of boys to do this; but select a man who has got a family to be a Deacon, whose wife can go with him, and assist him in administering to the needy in the ward.

These are simply my views in a few words on this subject, and always have been since I have reflected upon the doctrine that the fathers teach us in the Holy Scriptures. I will venture to say the view I take of the matter is not to be disputed or disproved by Scripture or reason.

I have no reasonable grounds upon which to say it was not the custom in ancient times for a man to have more than one wife, but every reason to believe that it was the custom among the Jews, from the days of Abraham to the days of the Apostles, for they were lineal descendants of Abraham, Isaac, and Jacob, all of whom taught and practised the doctrine of plurality of wives, and were revered by the whole Jewish nation, and it is but natural that they should have respected

Chapter 14

THE OFFICES AND DUTIES OF THE
AARONIC PRIESTHOOD

When the Aaronic Priesthood is conferred on a man or a boy, he is ordained to an office in that priesthood. Offices of the priesthood are called *appendages* to the priesthood (see D&C 84:29–30; 107:5). Each office carries duties and responsibilities that may be given to those who meet in priesthood groups or quorums. Each group or quorum is presided over by a group leader or quorum president who teaches the members their duties and asks them to fill assignments.

The offices in the Aaronic Priesthood are *deacon, teacher, priest,* and *bishop.* Some men join the Church or become active after they have passed the usual age to receive the offices of the priesthood. No matter what their age, they usually start as deacons and can be advanced to higher offices if they are worthy.

DEACON

When a boy has been baptized and confirmed a member of the Church and is worthy, he may be ordained to the office of deacon when he is twelve years old. The deacons are usually assigned to pass the sacrament to members of the Church, act as ushers, keep Church buildings and grounds in good order, act as messengers for priesthood leaders, and fulfill special assignments such as collecting fast offerings.

Gospel Principles, 1986 edition, p. 81. Copyright © 1978, 1979, 1981 Corporation of the President of The Church of Jesus Christ of Latter-day Saints.

shall sound. When we depart, we shall hail our mothers, fathers, friends, and all whom we love who have fallen asleep in Jesus. There will be no fear of mobs, persecutions, or malicious law-suits and arrests; but it will be an eternity of felicity.

A question may be asked—"Will mothers have their children in eternity?" Yes! yes! Mothers, you shall have your children; for they shall have eternal life; for their debt is paid. There is no damnation awaits them, for they are in the spirit. But as the child dies, so shall it rise from the dead, and be for ever living in the learning of God. It will never grow: it will still be the child, in the same precise form as it appeared before it died out of its mother's arms, but possessing all the intelligence of a God. Children dwell in the mansions of glory and exercise power, but appear in the same form as when on earth. Eternity is full of thrones, upon which dwell thousands of children reigning on thrones of glory, with not one cubit added to their stature.

I will leave this subject here, and make a few remarks on the subject of baptism. The baptism of water, without the baptism of fire and the Holy Ghost attending it, is of no use: they are necessary and inseparably connected. An individual must be born of water and the spirit in order to get into the kingdom of God. In the German, the text bears me out the same as the revelations which I have given and taught for the last fourteen years on that subject. I have the testimony to put in their teeth. My testimony has been true all the time. You will find it in the declaration of John the Baptist. [Reads from the German.] John says, "I baptise you with water; but when Jesus comes, who has the power (or keys), he shall administer the baptism of fire and the Holy Ghost." Great God! where is now all the sectarian world? And if

this testimony is true, they are all damned as clearly as anathema can do it. *I know the text is true.* I call upon all you Germans who know that it is true to say aye. (Loud shouts of aye.)

Alexander Campbell, how are you going to save people with water alone? For John said his baptism was good for nothing without the baptism of Jesus Christ. "Therefore, not leaving the principles of the doctrine of Christ, let us go on unto perfection, not laying again the foundation of repentance from dead works, and of faith toward God, of the doctrine of baptisms, and of laying on of hands, and of resurrection of the dead, and of eternal judgment. And this will we do, if God permit." (Heb. 6th chap., 1st to 3rd v.)

There is one God, one Father, one Jesus, one hope of our calling, one baptism. All these three baptisms only make one. Many talk of baptism not being essential to salvation: but this kind of teaching would lay the foundation of their damnation. I have the truth, and am at the defiance of the world to contradict me if they can.

I have now preached a little Latin, a little Hebrew, Greek, and German; and I have fulfilled all. I am not so big a fool as many have taken me to be. The Germans know that I read the German correctly.

Hear it, all ye ends of the earth—all ye priests, all ye sinners, and all men. Repent! repent! Obey the Gospel. Turn to God; for your religion won't save you, and you will be damned. I do not say how long. There have been remarks made concerning all men being redeemed from hell; but I say that those who sin against the Holy Ghost cannot be forgiven in this world or in the world to come: they shall die the second death. Those who commit the unpardonable sin are doomed to Gnolom, to dwell in hell, worlds without end.

Joseph Smith, April 6, 1844 (at a General Conference), *Journal of Discourses* 6:10.

is right here'' (John A. Widtsoe, comp., *Discourses of Brigham Young*, p. 376).

Where is the spirit world?

WHAT ARE SPIRITS LIKE?

Spirit beings have the same bodily form as mortals except that the spirit body is in perfect form (see Ether 3:16). Spirits carry with them from earth their same attitudes of devotion or antagonism toward things of righteousness (see Alma 34:34). They have the same appetites and desires that they had when they lived on earth.

All spirits are in adult form. They were adults before their mortal existence, and they are in adult form after death, even if they die as infants or children (see Joseph F. Smith, *Gospel Doctrine*, p. 455).

Read Ether 3:16. What do spirit bodies look like?

Gospel Principles, 1986 edition, p. 278. Copyright © 1978, 1979, 1981 Corporation of the President of The Church of Jesus Christ of Latter-day Saints.

false teacher, then, upon the same principle, we should be justified in taking away the life of every false teacher; and where would be the end of blood? and who would not be the sufferer?

But meddle not with any man for his religion; and all governments ought to permit every man to enjoy his religion unmolested. No man is authorized to take away life in consequence of difference of religion, which all laws and governments ought to tolerate and protect, right or wrong. Every man has a natural and, in our country, a constitutional right to be a false prophet as well as a true prophet. If I show, verily, that I have the truth of God, and show that ninety-nine out of every hundred professing religious ministers are false teachers, having no authority, while they pretend to hold the keys of God's kingdom on earth, and was to kill them because they are false teachers, it would deluge the whole world with blood.

I will prove that the world is wrong, by showing what God is. I am going to inquire after God; for I want you all to know him and to be familiar with him; and if I can bring you to a knowledge of him, all persecutions against me ought to cease. You will then know that I am his servant; for I speak as one having authority.

I will go back to the beginning, before the world was, to show what kind of a being God is. What sort of a being was God in the beginning? Open your ears and hear, all ye ends of the earth; for I am going to prove it to you by the Bible, and to tell you the designs of God in relation to the human race, and why he interferes with the affairs of man.

God himself was once as we are now, and is an exalted Man, and sits enthroned in yonder heavens. That is the great secret. If the vail was rent to-day, and the great God who holds this world in its orbit, and who upholds all worlds and all things by his power, was to make himself visible, —I say, if you were to see him to-day, you would see him like a man in form — like yourselves, in all the person, image, and very form as a man; for Adam was created in the very fashion, image, and likeness o God, and received instruction from, and walked, talked, and conversed with him, as one man talks and communes with another.

In order to understand the subject of the dead, for the consolation of those who mourn for the loss of their friends, it is necessary that we should understand the character and being of God, and how he came to be so; for I am going to tell you how God came to be God. We have imagined and supposed that God was God from all eternity, I will refute that idea, and will take away and do away the vail, so that you may see.

These are incomprehensible ideas to some; but they are simple. It is the first principle of the Gospel to know for a certainty the character of God and to know that we may converse with him as one man converses with another, and that he was once a man like us; yea, that God himself the Father of us all, dwelt on an earth the same as Jesus Christ himself did; and I will show it from the Bible. I wish I was in a suitable place to tell it, and that I had the trump of an archangel, so that I could tell the story in such a manner that persecution would cease for ever. What did Jesus say? (Mark it, Elder Rigdon.) The Scriptures inform us that Jesus said, "As the Father hath power in himself, even so hath the Son power" —to do what? Why, what the Father did. The answer is obvious— in a manner, to lay down his body and take it up again. Jesus, what are you doing to do? To lay down my life, as my Father did, and take it up again. Do you believe it? If you

Joseph Smith, April 6, 1844, *Journal of Discourses* 6:3.

crated to God and His Church? What can I produce? What will the book show? I prayed that I might, with my brethren, be spared to return and be allowed the privilege of consecrating to God my earthly goods. and felt a pleasure in dashing ahead, be the consequences what they might. Our prayers were answered, and I have, in part, complied with the dictates of conscience teaching this thing, so that when the books shall be opened, and another book opened, and the dead judged out of those things that are written in the books, I shall rejoice to see that the records will show my feelings towards the Church. Whatever earthly goods I possess, and what I am, are at the service and disposal of my brethren to advance the interests of the kingdom of God.

When I heard this morning the remarks that were made, all worldly interests looked like trash to me. I have laboured hard to lay a good foundation in the west for a settlement, but if what we have done must fall a sacrifice, so be it. We did what we thought was right, and tried to do considerable of it. The fact is, I count an inheritance in the kingdom of God greater than anything that this world can afford.

Let us remember what has been said to us to-day, and not forget it; and let us make our calling and election sure, and ask God Almighty to save us from every ill, except what He gives us strength to endure, that we may be accounted worthy to be crowned in His presence, which may He grant in the name of Jesus. Amen.

TO KNOW GOD IS ETERNAL LIFE — GOD THE FATHER OF OUR SPIRITS AND BODIES — THINGS CREATED SPIRITUALLY FIRST — ATONEMENT BY THE SHEDDING OF BLOOD.

A Discourse by President Brigham Young, Delivered in the Tabernacle, Great Salt Lake City, February 8, 1857.

I feel myself somewhat under obligations to come here and talk to the people, inasmuch as I have absented myself for some time, and others have occupied this stand.

Perhaps I will not talk to you long, but I desire to pursue some of the ideas that brother Cummings has just laid before you. I can testify that every word he has spoken is true, even to the advancement of the Saints at a " snail gallop." Though that is rather a novel expression, still it is true, as well as all the rest which he advanced.

The items that have been advanced are principles of real doctrine, whether you consider them so or not. It is one of the first principles of the doctrine of salvation to become acquaint-with our Father and our God. The Scriptures teach that this is eternal life, to " know Thee, the only true God, and Jesus Christ whom thou hast sent;" this is as much as to say that no man can enjoy or be prepared for eternal life without that knowledge.

You hear a great deal of preaching upon this subject; and when people

DOCTRINE AND COVENANTS

OF

THE CHURCH OF THE

LATTER DAY SAINTS:

CAREFULLY SELECTED

FROM THE REVELATIONS OF GOD,

AND COMPILED BY

JOSEPH SMITH Junior
OLIVER COWDERY,
SIDNEY RIGDON,
FREDERICK G. WILLIAMS,

[*Presiding Elders of said Church.*]

PROPRIETORS.

———————————

KIRTLAND, OHIO.

PRINTED BY F. G. WILLIAMS & CO.

FOR THE

PROPRIETORS.
....
1835.

Original 1835 edition of Doctrine and Covenants, title page.

knoweth save he that receiveth it. The new name is the key word.

12 I prophesy, in the name of the Lord God, that the commencement of the ªdifficulties which will cause much bloodshed previous to the coming of the Son of Man will be in South Carolina.

13 It may probably arise through the slave question. This a ªvoice declared to me, while I was praying earnestly on the subject, December 25th, 1832.

14 I was once praying very earnestly to know the time of the ªcoming of the Son of Man, when I heard a voice repeat the following:

15 Joseph, my son, if thou livest until thou art eighty-five years old, thou shalt see the face of the Son of Man; therefore ªlet this suffice, and trouble me no more on this matter.

16 I was left thus, without being able to decide whether this coming referred to the beginning of the millennium or to some previous appearing, or whether I should die and thus see his face.

17 I believe the coming of the Son of Man will not be any sooner than that time.

18 Whatever principle of ªintelligence we attain unto in this life, it will rise with us in the ᵇresurrection.

19 And if a person gains more ªknowledge and intelligence in this life through his ᵇdiligence and obedience than another, he will have so much the ʳadvantage in the world to come.

20 There is a ªlaw, irrevocably decreed in ᵇheaven before the foundations of this world, upon which all ʳblessings are predicated—

21 And when we obtain any ªblessing from God, it is by ᵇobedience to that law upon which it is predicated.

22 The ªFather has a ᵇbody of flesh and bones as tangible as man's; the Son also; but the Holy Ghost has not a body of flesh and bones, but is a personage of ʳSpirit. Were it not so, the Holy Ghost could not ᵈdwell in us.

23 A man may receive the ªHoly Ghost, and it may descend upon him and not ᵇtarry with him.

Today's Doctrine and Covenants 130:22. Copyright © 1981 Corporation of the President of The Church of Jesus Christ of Latter-day Saints.

Q. Where are the revelations to be found which give this relation of the attributes of God?

A. In the Old and New Testaments, and they are quoted in the fourth lecture, fifth, sixth, seventh, eighth, ninth, and tenth paragraphs.*

Q. Is the idea of the existence of those attributes, in the Deity, necessary in order to enable any rational being to exercise faith in him unto life and salvation?

A. It is.

Q. How do you prove it?

A. By the eleventh, twelfth, thirteenth fourteenth, fifteenth and sixteenth paragraphs in this lecture.*

Q. Does the idea of the existence of these attributes in the Deity, as far as his attributes are concerned, enable a rational being to exercise faith in him unto life and salvation?

A. It does.

Q. How do you prove it?

A. By the seventeenth and eighteenth paragraphs.*

Q. Have the Latter Day Saints as much authoity given them, through the revelation of the attributes of God, to exercise faith in him as the Former Day Saints had?

A. They have.

Q. How do you prove it?

A. By the nineteenth paragraph of this lecture.*

Note. Let the student turn and commit those paragraphs to memory.

LECTURE FIFTH.

Of Faith.

SECTION V.

1 In our former lectures we treated of the being, character, perfections and attributes of God. What we mean by perfections, is, the perfections which belong to all the attributes of his nature. We shall, in this lecture speak of the Godhead: we mean the Father, Son and Holy Spirit.

2 There are two personages who constitute the great, matchless, governing and supreme power over

all things—by whom all things were created and made, that are created and made, whether visible or invisible: whether in heaven, on earth, or in the earth, under the earth, or throughout the immensity of space —They are the Father and the Son: The Father being a personage of spirit, glory and power: possessing all perfection and fulness: The Son, who was in the bosom of the Father, a personage of tabernacle, made, or fashioned like unto man, or being in the form and likeness of man, or, rather, man was formed after his likeness, and in his image;—he is also the express image and likeness of the personage of the Father: possessing all the fulness of the Father, or, the same fulness with the Fathe; being begotten of him, and was ordained from before the foundation of the world to be a propitiation for the sins of all those who should believe on his name, and is called the Son because of the flesh—and descended in suffering below that which man can suffer, or, in other words, suffered greater sufferings, and was exposed to more powerful contradictions than any man can be. But notwithstanding all this, he kept the law of God, and remained without sin: Showing thereby that it is in the power of man to keep the law and remain also without sin. And also, that by him a righteous judgment might come upon all flesh, and that all who walk not in the law of God, may justly be condemned by the law, and have no excuse for their sins. And he being the only begotten of the Father, full of grace and truth, and having overcome, received a fulness of the glory of the Father—possessing the same mind with the Father, which mind is the Holy Spirit, that bears record of the Father and the Son, and these three are one, or in other words, these three constitute the great, matchless, governing and supreme power over all things: by whom all things were created and made, that were created and made: and these three

Original 1835 edition of Doctrine and Covenants, "Lecture Fifth of Faith," 5:2 (pp. 52–53).

the west; and as it gives particulars we insert it, deferring further remarks till a future number.—[*Editor of the Star.*]

Liberty, May 1, 1834.

DEAR BRETHREN:—There are great moves in the west. Last week an alarm was spread in Jackson county, the seat of iniquity and bloodshed, that the "Mormons" were crossing the Missouri, to take possession of their lands, and nearly all the county turned out, "prepared for war," on Saturday, and on Sunday took the field, near old McGees, above Blue. But no "Mormons" came; neither did Arthur go over to see about his *spilt whiskey*, so that the scene closed with burning our houses, or many of them. Our people had about one hundred and seventy buildings in Jackson, and a bonfire of nearly all of them, at once, must have made a light large enough to have glared on the dark deed and cup of iniquity running over, at midnight.

The crisis has come: All that will not take up arms with the mob and prepare to fight the "Mormons," have to leave Jackson county.

I understand some have left the county because they refused to fight an innocent people. It is said the mob will hold a "general muster" this week for the purpose of learning *who is who*. They begin to slip over the Missouri and commit small depredations upon our brethren settled near the river, as we have reason to believe.

It is said to be enough to shock the stoutest heart to witness the drinking, swearing, and ravings of the most of the mob: nothing but the power of God can stop them in their latter day crusade against the church of Christ. Our brethren are very industrious in putting in spring crops; and they are generally in good health and the faithful in strong faith of a glorious hereafter.

I remain yours, &c,
W. W. PHELPS.

Communicated.

Kirtland, Ohio, May 3, 1834.

MINUTES of a Conference of the Elders of the church of Christ, which church was organized in the township of Fayette, Seneca county, New-York, on the 6th of April. A. D. 1830.

The Conference came to order, and JOSEPH SMITH JN. was chosen Moderator, and FREDERICK G. WILLIAMS and OLIVER COWDERY, were appointed clerks.

After prayer the Conference proceeded to discuss the subject of names and appellations, when a motion was made by SIDNEY RIGDON, and seconded by NEWEL K. WHITNEY, that this church be known hereafter by the name of THE CHURCH OF THE LATTER DAY SAINTS. Appropriate remarks were delivered by some of the members, after which the motion was put by the Moderator, and passed by unanimous voice.

Resolved that this Conference recommend to the Conferences and Churches abroad, in making out and transmitting Minutes of their proceedings, such minutes and proceedings be made out under the above title.

Resolved that these Minutes be signed by the Moderator and Clerks, and

---

scription. The low price of the Star will enable every individual, if disposed, to become a subscriber. From our brethren in the ministry we have a right to expect an unceasing exertion to increase the spread of this paper, as they will often find by so doing, that where they introduce the Star, frequent doors are opened and they kindly received, deep rooted malice gives way, and the public is thus prepared to give them a hearing without abuse, which otherwise might not have been. As the work spreads the Star will continue to be more interesting, and as the time draws nigh when desolations are to cover the wicked and envelop the nations in one universal calamity, we can only persuade men to turn to God that they may stand unmoved with his saints, when deliverance is not to be found except in mount Zion, and in Jerusalem, and in the remnant whom the Lord shall call.—[*Editor.*]

THE GATHERING.

WHAT wond'rous things we now behold,
Which were declar'd from days of old
By prophets, who in vision clear
Beheld those glories from afar.

The visions which the God,
Confirm'd by his unchanging word,
That to the ages then unborn
His greatest work he would perform.

The second time he'd set his hand
To gather Isr'el to their land,
Fulfil the cov'nants he had made,
And pour his blessings on their head.

When Moab's remnant, long oppress'd,
Should gather home and greatly blest:
And Ammons children, scatter'd wide,
Return with joy, in peace abide.

While Elam's race a feeble band,
Receive a share in the blest land:
And Gentiles, all their power display
To hasten on the glorious day.

Then Ephraim's sons, a warlike race,
Shall haste in peace and see their rest,
And earth's remotest parts abound,
With joys of everlasting sound.

Assyria's captives, long since lost,
In splendor come a num'rous host;
Egypt's waters fill'd with fear,
Their power feel and disappear.

Yes, Abram's children now shall be
Like sand in number by the sea;
While kindreds, tongues, and nations all
Combine, to make the numbers full.

The dawning of that day has come,
See! Abram's sons are gath'ring home,
And daughters too, with joyful lays,
Are hast'ning here to join in praise!

O God, our Father, and our King,
Prepare our voices and our theme:
Let all our pow'rs in one combine
To sing thy praise in songs divine.

The Evening and the Morning Star

IS PUBLISHED EVERY MONTH AT

KIRTLAND, GEAUGA COUNTY, OHIO,

BY F. G. WILLIAMS & CO.

O. COWDERY, Editor.

THE PRICE IS ONE DOLLAR FOR A YEAR IN ADVANCE, EXCEPT SPECIAL CONTRACTS ARE MADE. EVERY PERSON THAT SENDS US $10, CURRENT MONEY, SHALL BE ENTITLED TO A PAPER FOR A YEAR, GRATIS. ALL LETTERS TO THE EDITOR, OR PUBLISHER, MUST BE POST PAID.

May 3.—Kirtland.

*Minutes of a Conference of the Elders of the Church of Christ, which Church was organized in the township of Fayette, Seneca county, New York, on the 6th of April, A.D. 1830.**

President Joseph Smith, Jun., was chosen moderator, and Frederick G. Williams and Oliver Cowdery were appointed clerks.

After prayer, the conference proceeded to discuss the subject of

names and appellations, when a motion was made by Sidney Rigdon, and seconded by Newel K. Whitney, that this Church be known hereafter by the name of "The Church of the Latter-day Saints." Remarks were made by the members, after which the motion passed by unanimous vote.

"Resolved, that this conference recommend to the conferences and churches abroad, that in making out and transmitting minutes of their proceedings, such minutes and proceedings be made out under the above title.

"Resolved, that these minutes be signed by the moderator and clerks, and published in the *Evening and Morning Star.*

JOSEPH SMITH, JUN., Moderator.

FREDERICK G. WILLIAMS, } Clerks.
OLIVER COWDERY,

History of the Church 2:62–63. Copyright © 1978 Deseret Book Company.

CHURCH OF CHRIST.
    See CHRIST, CHURCH, CHURCH OF JESUS CHRIST OF LATTER-DAY SAINTS, MORMONS. One or more of the names of Christ has always been used in the formal name of the Church. The revelation commanding the Prophet to organize the Church in this dispensation speaks of it as the *Church of Christ.* (D. & C. 20:1.) Similar usage is found

Apostle Bruce McConkie, *Mormon Doctrine*, 1979 ed., p. 136. Copyright © 1966 Bookcraft, Inc.

SECTION CI.

MARRIAGE.

1 According to the custom of all civilized nations, marriage is regulated by laws and ceremonies: therefore we believe, that all marriages in this church of Christ of Latter Day Saints, should be solemnized in a public meeting, or feast, prepared for that purpose: and that the solemnization should be performed by a presiding high priest, high priest, bishop, elder, or priest, not even prohibiting those persons who are desirous to get married, of being married by other authority. We believe that it is not right to prohibit members of this church from marrying out of the church, if it be their determination so to do, but such persons will be considered weak in the faith of our Lord and Savior Jesus Christ.

2 Marriage should be celebrated with prayer and thanksgiving; and at the solemnization, the persons to be married, standing together, the man on the right, and the woman on the left, shall be addressed, by the person officiating, as he shall be directed by the holy Spirit; and if there be no legal objections, he shall say, calling each by their names: "You both mutually agree to be each other's companion, husband and wife, observing the legal rights belonging to this condition; that is, keeping yourselves wholly for each other, and from all others, during your lives." And when they have answered "Yes," he shall pronounce them "husband and wife" in the name of the Lord Jesus Christ, and by virtue of the laws of the country and authority vested in him: "may God add his blessings and keep you to fulfill your covenants from henceforth and forever. Amen."

3 The clerk of every church should keep a record of all marriages, solemnized in his branch.

4 All legal contracts of marriage made before a person is baptized into this church, should be held sacred and fulfilled. Inasmuch as this church of Christ has been reproached with the crime of fornication, and polygamy: we declare that we believe, that one man should have one wife; and one woman, but one husband, except in case of death, when either is at liberty to marry again. It is not right to persuade a woman to be baptized contrary to the will of her husband, neither is it lawful to influence her to leave her husband. All children are bound by law to obey their parents; and to influence them to embrace any religious faith, or be baptized, or leave their parents without their consent, is unlawful and unjust. We believe that all persons who exercise control over their fellow

SECTION 132

Revelation given through Joseph Smith the Prophet, at Nauvoo, Illinois, recorded July 12, 1843, relating to the new and everlasting covenant, including the eternity of the marriage covenant, as also plurality of wives. HC 5: 501–507. Although the revelation was recorded in 1843, it is evident from the historical records that the doctrines and principles involved in this revelation had been known by the Prophet since 1831.

Doctrine and Covenants, 1990 printing, section 132 introduction. Copyright © 1981 Corporation of the President of The Church of Jesus Christ of Latter-day Saints.

and doctrine of their having many ᵃwives and ᵇconcubines—

2 Behold, and lo, I am the Lord thy God, and will answer thee as touching this matter.

3 Therefore, ᵃprepare thy heart to receive and ᵇobey the instructions which I am about to give unto you; for all those who have this law revealed unto them must obey the same.

4 For behold, I reveal unto you a new and an everlasting ᵃcovenant; and if ye abide not that covenant, then are ye ᵇdamned; for no one can ʳreject this covenant and be permitted to enter into my glory.

5 For all who will have a ᵃblessing at my hands shall abide the ᵇlaw which was appointed for that blessing, and the conditions thereof, as were instituted from before the foundation of the world.

that too most holy, by ᶠrevelation and commandment through the medium of mine anointed, whom I have appointed on the earth to hold this ᵍpower (and I have appointed unto my servant Joseph to hold this ʰpower in the last days, and there is never but one on the earth at a time on whom this power and the ⁱkeys of this priesthood are conferred), are of no efficacy, virtue, or force in and after the resurrection from the dead; for all contracts that are not made unto this end have an end when men are dead.

8 Behold, mine house is a house of ᵃorder, saith the Lord God, and not a house of confusion.

9 Will I ᵃaccept of an offering, saith the Lord, that is not made in my name?

10 Or will I receive at your hands that which I have not ᵃappointed?

Doctrine and Covenants 132:4. Copyright © 1981 Corporation of the President of The Church of Jesus Christ of Latter-day Saints.

12

Scripture Changes

Most Mormons hold their unique scriptures—the Book of Mormon, Doctrine and Covenants, Pearl of Great Price—in higher regard than the Bible, since they have been taught that there were "many plain and precious things taken away" from the Bible (1 Nephi 13:28). But does this view of matters conform to the facts? Has the Bible suffered alteration? Have the uniquely Mormon scriptures been preserved intact?

To the contrary, the Dead Sea Scrolls and other ancient manuscripts verify that the Bible we have today has survived thousands of years essentially unchanged. A thorough discussion of the completeness and reliability of the Bible can be found in such books as *Evidence That Demands a Verdict* by Josh McDowell and *The New Testament Documents—Are They Reliable?* by F. F. Bruce. But the Mormon scriptures Doctrine and Covenants and the Book of Mormon differ considerably today from the original editions published less than two centuries ago. In fact, as early as 1898 researcher Lamoni Call published the results of his critical study under the title *2000 Changes in the Book of Mormon.* And current researchers Jerald and Sandra Tanner have published a volume titled *3,913 Changes in the Book of Mormon*, a photomechanical reprint of the original 1830 edition of the Book of Mormon marked to show alterations made since then.[1]

1. The Tanners' study and a reprint of Lamoni Call's work are both available from Utah Lighthouse Ministry, P.O. Box 1884, Salt Lake City, UT 84110.

Many of the changes made in the Book of Mormon are relatively insignificant and have little impact on the message presented. But even these call into question Joseph Smith's claim that "a voice from out of the bright light above us" told him, "These plates . . . have been translated by the power of God. The translation of them which you have seen is correct . . ." (*History of the Church*, vol. 1, pp. 54–55). Mormon historian B. H. Roberts's alleged verification from Smith's handwritten manuscript affirms that the first edition of the Book of Mormon was "singularly free from typographical errors" (*Defense of the Faith*, p. 279). If the handwritten manuscript was correct and the printed version free of errors, why have LDS leaders since then made so many alterations in it?

Far from being merely cosmetic, a number of these alterations have significantly changed the meaning of the text, quite radically in some cases. Consider, for example, 1 Nephi, chapter 11, verses 18 and 21. Besides numbering the verses and dividing the chapters differently, current editions of the Book of Mormon insert the phrase *the Son of* in both verses. The first edition presented Mary as "the mother of God, after the manner of the flesh" and Jesus as "the Lamb of God, yea, even the Eternal Father!" But, as now revised, Mary is made "the mother of *the Son of* God, after the manner of the flesh" (v. 18) and Jesus is made "the Lamb of God, yea, even *the Son of* the Eternal Father!"[2] (v. 21, *emphasis added*), a significant change indeed. The full import of this alteration comes to light when it is appreciated that Mormonism became polytheistic *after* publication of the Book of Mormon, and that the LDS Church today teaches that Jesus Christ and the Eternal Father (Elohim) are two separate and distinct Gods, each having a body of flesh and bones (Doctrine and Covenants 130:22). So the verse in the original Book of Mormon identifying Jesus as the Eternal Father was altered to conform to the sect's changing theology.

In the previous chapter we pointed out major changes in Mormon theology that were accomplished by removal of portions of Doctrine and Covenants that had proclaimed God the Father to be "a personage of spirit" and that limited the Godhead to two

2. Similar changes are also found at 1 Nephi 11:32 and 13:40.

personages instead of three. In all, a seventy-page section, "Lectures on Faith," was quietly removed from Doctrine and Covenants in 1921. Although this material had been approved by a unanimous vote of a General Assembly of the LDS Church (page 252 in the 1835 Doctrine and Covenants), there appears to be no evidence of a similar vote to eliminate it.

Individual revelations allegedly received by Joseph Smith, Jr., and recorded in Doctrine and Covenants have also been revised, in spite of later Mormon Apostle Joseph Fielding Smith's assertion to the contrary: "There was no need for eliminating, changing, or adjusting any part to make it fit; but each new revelation on doctrine and priesthood fitted in its place perfectly" (*Doctrines of Salvation*, vol. 1, p. 170). This is manifestly not the case in regard to the revelation Joseph Smith, Jr., allegedly received at Harmony, Pennsylvania, in April 1829, when he and his associate Oliver Cowdery inquired whether the apostle John had tarried in the flesh or had died. Included originally as chapter 6 of the 1833 *Book of Commandments* and today as section 7 of Doctrine and Covenants, the revelation purports to be a translation of words written on parchment by John himself. As printed in 1833 the opening verses show John asking the Lord to "give me power that I may bring souls unto thee." But today's version expands this considerably, having John ask also for "power over death, that I may live and bring souls unto thee" (v. 2) and having the Lord tell Peter regarding John and himself, "I will make him as flaming fire and a ministering angel," and "I will make thee to minister for him and for thy brother James; and unto you three I will give this power and the keys of this ministry until I come" (vv. 6–7). So this basis for the claim that Peter, James, and John later appeared to Joseph Smith and restored the Melchizedek Priesthood was not found in the revelation as originally published but was added afterwards.

Likewise was the Lord's alleged declaration in today's Doctrine and Covenants 5:4–6 that power "to translate the plates" of the Book of Mormon was merely "the first gift I bestowed upon" Joseph Smith, to be followed by his being "ordained to go forth" and preach. As originally published in the *Book of Commandments* the same revelation declared that Smith "has a gift to translate the book" but that he "shall pretend to no other gift, for I will grant him no other gift" (4:2). To allow for the additional gift of preaching, the revised revelation has the Lord say Smith "should pretend to no other gift *until my purpose is fulfilled in this; for I will grant unto you no other gift until it is finished*" *(emphasis added).* The added words thus turn the Lord's alleged statement around to mean the opposite of what he was originally quoted as saying.

Although we could fill another book with changes the LDS Church has made in the Book of Mormon and in Doctrine and Covenants, the examples cited above suffice to prove that there have been significant additions, deletions, and alterations so as to change the meaning and the doctrinal import of entire passages. Persons who have been taught to downplay the Bible while giving greater credence to the unique scriptures of Mormonism owe it to themselves, and to God, to make further investigation. "For all flesh is as grass, and all the glory of man as the flower of grass. The grass withereth, and the flower thereof falleth away: But the word of the Lord endureth for ever. And this is the word which by the gospel is preached unto you" (1 Peter 1:24–25).

unto me, Knowest thou the condescention of God? And I said unto him, I know that he loveth his children; nevertheless, I do not know the meaning of all things. And he said unto me, Behold, the virgin which thou seest, is the mother of God, after the manner of the flesh.

And it came to pass that I beheld that she was carried away in the spirit; and after that she had been carried away in the spirit for the space of a time, the angel spake unto me, saying, look! And I looked and beheld the virgin again, bearing a child in her arms. And the angel said unto me, behold the Lamb of God, yea, even the Eternal Father! Knowest thou the meaning of the tree which thy father saw? And I answered him, saying: Yea, it is the love of God, which sheddeth itself abroad in the hearts of the children of men; wherefore, it is the most desirable above all things. And he spake unto me, saying, Yea, and the most joyous to the soul. And after that he had

First Book of Nephi, chapter 3, page 25, Book of Mormon, 1830 (First edition)

1 NEPHI 11:9–25 20

looked and beheld a tree; and it was like unto the *tree which my father had seen; and the *beauty thereof was far beyond, yea, exceeding of all beauty; and the *whiteness thereof did exceed the whiteness of the driven snow.

9 And it came to pass after I had seen the tree, I said unto the Spirit: I beheld thou hast shown unto me the tree which is *precious above all.

10 And he said unto me: What desirest thou?

11 And I said unto him: To know the *interpretation thereof—for I spake unto him as a man speaketh; for I beheld that he was in the *form of a man; yet nevertheless, I knew that it was the Spirit of the Lord; and he spake unto me as a man speaketh with another.

12 And it came to pass that he said

17 And I said unto him: I know that he loveth his children; nevertheless, I do not know the meaning of all things.

18 And he said unto me: Behold, the *virgin whom thou seest is the *mother of the Son of God, after the manner of the flesh.

19 And it came to pass that I beheld that she was carried away in the Spirit; and after she had been carried away in the *Spirit for the space of a time the angel spake unto me, saying: Look!

20 And I looked and beheld the virgin again, bearing a *child in her arms.

21 And the angel said unto me: Behold the *Lamb of God, yea, even the *Son of the Eternal *Father! Knowest thou the meaning of the *tree which thy father saw?

1 Nephi 11:18-21, Book of Mormon, 1981

1 Nephi 11:18–21 in Book of Mormon, 1981 edition, and chapter 3, page 25 in original 1830 edition (first edition). Copyright © 1981 Corporation of the President of The Church of Jesus Christ of Latter-day Saints.

CHAPTER VI.

1 *A Revelation given to Joseph and Oliver, in Harmony, Pennsylvania, April, 1829, when they desired to know whether John, the beloved disciple, tarried on earth. Translated from parchment, written and hid up by himself.*

AND the Lord said unto me, John my beloved, what desirest thou? and I said Lord, give unto me power that I may bring souls unto thee.— And the Lord said unto me: Verily, verily I say unto thee, because thou desiredst this, thou shalt tarry till I come in my glory:

2 And for this cause, the Lord said unto Peter:— If I will that he tarry till I come, what is that to thee? for he desiredst of me that he might bring souls unto me: but thou desiredst that thou might speedily come unto me in my kingdom: I say unto thee, Peter, this was a good desire, but my beloved has undertaken a greater work.

3 Verily I say unto you, ye shall both have according to your desires, for ye both joy in that which ye have desired.

Book of Commandments, Chapter VI, Page 18, as first published in 1833.

1–3, John the Beloved shall live until the Lord comes; 4–8, Peter, James, and John hold gospel keys.

AND the Lord said unto me: John, my *beloved, what *desirest thou? For if you shall ask what you will, it shall be granted unto you.

2 And I said unto him: Lord, give unto me *power over *death, that I may live and bring souls unto thee.

3 And the Lord said unto me: Verily, verily, I say unto thee, because thou desirest this thou shalt *tarry until I come in my *glory, and shalt *prophesy before nations, kindreds, tongues and people.

4 And for this cause the Lord said unto Peter: If I will that he tarry till I come, what is that to thee? For he desired of me that he might bring *souls unto me, but thou de-

siredst that thou mightest speedily come unto me in my *kingdom.

5 I say unto thee, Peter, this was a good desire; but my beloved has desired that he might do more, or a greater *work yet among men than what he has before done.

6 Yea, he has undertaken a greater work; therefore I will make him as flaming fire and a *ministering angel; he shall minister for those who shall be *heirs of salvation who dwell on the earth.

7 And I will make thee to minister for him and for thy brother James; and unto you three I will *give this power and the *keys of this ministry until I come.

8 Verily I say unto you, ye shall both have according to your desires, for ye both *joy in that which ye have desired.

Doctrine & Covenants, Section 7, 1981 Edition.

Doctrine and Covenants, 1981 edition, Section 7, contrasted with *Book of Commandments,* chapter VI, page 18, published in 1833. Copyright © 1981 Corporation of the President of The Church of Jesus Christ of Latter-day Saints.

2 And now, behold, this shall you say unto him: —I the Lord am God, and I have given these things unto my servant Joseph, and I have commanded him that he should stand as a witness of these things, nevertheless I have caused him that he should enter into a covenant with me, that he should not show them except I command him, and he has no power over them except I grant it unto him; and he has a gift to translate the book, and I have commanded him that he shall pretend to no other gift, for I will grant him no other gift.

3 And verily I say unto you, that wo shall come unto the inhabitants of the earth, if they will not hearken unto my words, for, behold, if they will not believe my words, they would not believe my servant Joseph, if it were possible that he could show

Book of Commandments 4:2, printed in 1833, Independence, Missouri.

2 And now, behold, this shall you say unto him—he who spake unto you, said unto you: I, the Lord, am God, and have given these things unto you, my servant Joseph Smith, Jun., and have commanded you that you should stand as a *witness of these things;

3 And I have caused you that you should enter into a *covenant with me, that you should not *show them except to those *persons to whom I commanded you; and you have no *power over them except I grant it unto you.

4 And you have a gift to *translate the plates; and this is the first gift that I bestowed upon you; and I have commanded that you should pretend to no other gift until my purpose is fulfilled in this; for I will

grant unto you no other gift until it is finished.

5 Verily, I say unto you, that *woe shall come unto the inhabitants of the earth if they will not *hearken unto my words;

6 For hereafter you shall be *ordained and go forth and deliver my *words unto the children of men.

7 Behold, if they will not *believe my words, they would not believe you, my servant Joseph, if it were possible that you should show them all these things which I have committed unto you.

8 Oh, this *unbelieving and *stiffnecked generation—mine *anger is kindled against them.

9 Behold, verily I say unto you, I have *reserved those things which I have entrusted unto you, my

5 1a D&C 5: 23 (23–24); JS-H 1: 61.

4a D&C 3: 12; 6: 25 (25, 28).

b Morm. 8: 33.
TG Haughtiness;

Doctrine & Covenants 5:4, 1989 (Columns shifted to save space).

Doctrine and Covenants 5:4, 6 in 1989 edition, contrasted with *Book of Commandments* 4:2–3, published in 1833. Copyright © 1981 Corporation of the President of The Church of Jesus Christ of Latter-day Saints.

13

Strange Teachings

Second only to Joseph Smith in importance is his successor Brigham Young, who brought the Mormon Church to Utah and commenced building the organization that we find at Salt Lake City today. Was Brigham Young truly what he claimed to be? On the other hand, if the LDS Church did not teach the truth under the leadership of Brigham Young, could it be expected to teach the truth today? Rather than answer these questions for your Mormon loved one, invite him or her to consider the material presented in this chapter and reach a conclusion based on the evidence.

Strange as it may seem, Brigham Young taught that the first man Adam brought animals and plants to earth from other planets. The Bible, of course, teaches at Genesis 2:7 that "the LORD God formed man of the dust of the ground, and breathed into his nostrils the breath of life; and man became a living soul." The apostle Paul adds his testimony to the truthfulness of this account of creation: "And so it is written, The first man Adam was made a living soul. . . . The first man is of the earth, earthy" (1 Cor. 15:45–47). But Brigham Young denies this, flatly contradicting the Bible:

> Though we have it in history that our father Adam was made of the dust of this earth, and that he knew nothing about his God previous to being made here, yet it is not so; and when we learn the

truth we shall see and understand that he helped to make this world, and was the chief manager in that operation.

He was the person who brought the animals and the seeds from other planets to this world, and brought a wife with him and stayed here. You may read and believe what you please as to what is found written in the Bible. Adam was made from the dust of an earth, but not from the dust of this earth (Brigham Young, *Journal of Discourses*, April 20, 1856, vol. 3, p. 319).

In these few words Brigham Young not only (1) denies the Bible's inspired account of Adam's creation but also (2) says Adam "brought a wife with him" to this planet, thus contradicting what Genesis 2:22 says about Eve; (3) says Adam "brought the animals and the seeds from other planets," thus negating more of the Genesis account; and (4) places Adam as "the chief manager" in the creation of the world.

Well, then, just who did Brigham Young believe Adam to be, if Adam helped create this world? The answer is found in another of the sermons this Mormon Prophet gave in his official capacity as God's spokesman to the Church of Jesus Christ of Latter-day Saints. On April 9, 1852, at General Conference[1] Brigham Young shocked Mormons and the world with his oft-quoted (or misquoted as Mormons would say) Adam-God discourse, (published in *Journal of Discourses*, vol. 1:50–51 and in *Millennial Star*, vol. 15, November 26, 1853, pp. 769–70). The heading in *Millennial Star* and *Journal of Discourses* 1:46 reads "ADAM, Our Father and Our GOD." Page 50 announces this new teaching:

When our father Adam came into the garden of Eden, he came into it with a *celestial body*, and brought Eve, *one of his wives*, with him. He helped to make and organize this world. He is MICHAEL, *the Archangel*, the ANCIENT OF DAYS! about whom holy men have written and spoken—HE *is our* FATHER *and our* GOD, *and the only God with whom* WE *have to do*. Every man upon the earth, professing Christians or non-professing, must hear it, and *will know it sooner or later*. . . . When the Virgin Mary conceived the child Jesus, the Father had begotten him in his own likeness. He was *not*

1. See footnote 3 in chapter 8, "Gods and Goddesses."

begotten by the Holy Ghost. And who is the Father? He is the first of the human family [emphasis in original].

A part of this discourse on page 51 not usually quoted is the following:

Now let all who may hear these doctrines, pause before they make light of them, or treat them with indifference, for they will prove their salvation or damnation.

Note the word *doctrines*. Brigham Young taught this as doctrine, not as a casual personal opinion. Note, too, that he said these doctrines "will prove their salvation or damnation." This Adam-God teaching was considered very important by Brigham Young. He taught that Adam was not only our God but also the father of our spirits, that Jesus was his firstborn spirit and the *only begotten* of Adam in the flesh.

Mormons confronted with this information often claim that *Journal of Discourses* 1:50–51 was transcribed incorrectly, so as not to have recorded Brigham Young's actual words. But the fact that his sermon was duplicated word for word eighteen months later in the *Millennial Star* furnishes a second witness that this really is what he said. In fact, Brigham Young consistently taught this doctrine as recorded in other sermons of his. It was believed by his followers and recorded in their diaries and journals. It was disputed by only one (Orson Pratt) of the General Authorities or top leaders of the Mormon Church during Brigham Young's reign. And eventually even Orson Pratt fell into line.

A full twenty years after making the above statements Brigham Young was still preaching the same thing. On June 18, 1873, *The Deseret News* published one of his clearest talks on this subject (p. 308, col. 4):

How much unbelief exists in the minds of the Latter-day Saints in regard to one particular doctrine which I revealed to them and which God revealed to me—namely that Adam is our Father and our God. . . . Our Father Adam helped to make this earth, it was created expressly for him. . . . He brought one of his wives with him, and she was called Eve.

In column 5 of this article Brigham Young continues:

"Why was Adam called Adam?" He was the first man on the earth, and its framer and maker. He with the help of his brethren, brought it into existence. Then he said, "I want my children who are in the spirit world to come and live here. I once dwelt upon an earth something like this, in a mortal state. I was faithful. I received my crown and exaltation. I have the privilege of extending my work, and to its increase there will be no end. I want my children that were born to me in the spirit world to come here and take tabernacles of flesh, that their spirits may have a house, a tabernacle or dwelling place as mine has. . . ."

Yes, unbelievable as it may seem, Brigham Young taught that Adam is God, the father of our "spirits"—"the only God with whom we have to do."

Other Mormon leaders joined him in proclaiming the same thing: "I have learned by experience that there is but one God that pertains to this people, and He is the God that pertains to this earth—the first man. That first man sent his own Son to redeem the world . . ." (Heber C. Kimball, *Journal of Discourses*, 1856, vol. 4, p. 1). Also: "'Adam is our Father and God. He is the God of the earth.' So says Brigham Young. Adam is the great archangel of this creation. He is Michael. He is the Ancient of Days. He is the father of our elder brother, Jesus Christ, the father of him who shall also come as Messiah to reign. He is the father of the spirits as well as the tabernacles of the sons and daughters of man, Adam" (Edward Tullidge, *The Women of Mormondom*, 1877, p. 179).

In fairness to modern-day Mormons, it should be said that most of them neither know of nor believe in the Adam-God doctrine. Although Brigham Young persisted in teaching it for more than twenty years, his successors at the head of the LDS Church have done their best to cover up the facts, pushing Adam-God "under the rug," so to speak. It has not been officially taught since the turn of the century, and in 1976 the twelfth Mormon President and Prophet, Spencer W. Kimball, denounced it strongly as false doctrine (*Church News*, October 9, 1976). When referred to at all today it is called the Adam-God *theory*.

The primary argument of Mormons who do not accept the Adam-God theory or doctrine is that it is not scriptural; and those who do accept the fact that Brigham Young actually taught it reject it because it was not presented to the membership for a "common consent" vote. However, a close look at the following Mormon canonized scripture verses reveals that the doctrine was already in Mormon scripture and therefore a membership vote was not required: "And also with Michael, or Adam, the father of all, the prince of all, the ancient of days" (Doctrine and Covenants 27:11, given August 1830 through Joseph Smith). "Spring Hill is named by the Lord Adam-ondi-Ahman, because, said he, it is the place where Adam shall come to visit his people, or the Ancient of Days shall sit, as spoken of by Daniel the prophet" (Doctrine and Covenants 116:1, given May 1838 through Joseph Smith).

This last verse, Doctrine and Covenants 116:1, says that Adam is the Ancient of Days spoken of by Daniel the prophet. And comparison of the references to the Ancient of Days at Daniel 7:9, 13–14, 22 with Revelation chapters 7 and 20 makes it clear that the Ancient of Days is "our God which sitteth upon the throne" (Rev. 7:10). So, Brigham Young was simply verbalizing a doctrine already found in Mormon scripture by implication.

Further supporting the above references is a newer "revelation" on the same subject: "Among the great and mighty ones who were assembled in this vast congregation of the righteous were Father Adam, the Ancient of Days and father of all" (Doctrine and Covenants 138:38, given October 1918 through Joseph Fielding Smith).

This is a very good topic for Christians to discuss with Mormons or with "investigators" (persons studying with missionaries to learn Mormonism). Be aware, though, that the LDS Church claims this is a false doctrine made up by enemies of the Church. If you begin with the verses[2] in Daniel chapter 7 and ask who is sitting on the throne, more than likely a Mormon will answer "God." (If he or she does not, then walk him through the items in the footnote.) Next, turn to the parallel passages in Revelation cited above. When he or she is fully convinced that this is God on the throne, then together look up the Mormon scriptures in

2. Footnotes in the 1979 edition of the Mormon Church's King James Bible under Daniel 7:9c, 13a, and 22a list these as cross references: Doctrine and Covenants 138:38, TG [Topical Guide] Adam; Rev. 11:15, TG Jesus Christ, Second Coming of; Jesus Christ, Son of Man; Doctrine and Covenants 27:11; 116:1. So the person sitting on the throne in Daniel is the person sitting on the throne in Revelation. And in Revelation it is "our God which sitteth upon the throne" (Rev. 1:4; 3:21; 7:10, 15; 14:5; 22:1).

Doctrine and Covenants that say that the Ancient of Days is
Adam.[3] If possible, show photocopies of the pertinent Brigham
Young discourses in context; if you simply quote a portion, you
will be accused of taking it out of context. The Mormon has to
see it for himself.

3. Note also that the LDS *Bible Dictionary* under "Resurrection" on page 761 says that
"a resurrection means to become immortal, without blood, yet with a body of flesh and
bone." Then under "Fall of Adam" on page 670 it says, "Before the fall, Adam and Eve had
physical bodies but no blood." Thus the *Dictionary*'s description of Adam before the fall
fits that of a resurrected being and so supports the Adam-God doctrine of Brigham Young.

if it is only to the extent of a hair's breadth. And if he cannot keep a person this side the Gospel line, he will walk with that individual on the line and strive to push him over.

That is so invariably the case that people need eyes to see, and understanding to know how to discriminate between the things of God and the things that are not of Him. Will this people learn? I am happy and joyful, I am thankful, and can say of a truth, brethren and sisters, that the manifestations of goodness from this people are not to be compared, in my opinion, with those from any other people upon the face of the whole earth since the days of Enoch.

Old Israel, in all their travels, wanderings, exercises, powers, and keys of the Priesthood, never came nigh enough to the path this people have walked in to see them in their obedience that was and is required by the Gospel. Yet there are thousands of weaknesses and overt acts in some of this people, which render us more or less obnoxious to each other.

Still, you may search all the history extant of the children of Israel, or that of any people that ever lived on the face of the earth since the days of Enoch, and I very much doubt, taking that people with their traditions, and comparing them with this mixed multitude from the different nations now in the world with our traditions, whether you would find a people from the days of Enoch until now that could favorably compare with this people in their willingness to obey the Gospel, and to go all lengths to build up the kingdom of God.

I have said a great many times, and repeat it now, and whether I am mistaken or not I will leave for the future to determine, and though, as I do, Joseph when living reproved the people, that I believe with all my heart that the people who gathered around Enoch, and lived with him and built up his City, when they had travelled the same length of time in their experience as this people have, were not as far advanced in the things of the kingdom of God.

Make your own comparisons between the two people, think of the traditions of the two. How many nations were there in the days of Enoch? The very men who were associated with him had been with Adam; they knew him and his children, and had the privilege of talking with God. Just think of it.

Though we have it in history that our father Adam was made of the dust of this earth, and that he knew nothing about his God previous to being made here, yet it is not so; and when we learn the truth we shall see and understand that he helped to make this world, and was the chief manager in that operation.

He was the person who brought the animals and the seeds from other planets to this world, and brought a wife with him and stayed here. You may read and believe what you please as to what is found written in the Bible. Adam was made from the dust of an earth, but not from the dust of this earth. He was made as you and I are made, and no person was ever made upon any other principle.

Do you not suppose that he was acquainted with his associates, who came and helped to make this earth? Yes, they were just as familiar with each other as we are with our children and parents.

Suppose a number of our sons were going to Carson Valley to build houses, open farms, and erect mills and workshops, and that we should say to them that we wish them to stay there five years, and that then we will come and visit them, when I go there will they be afraid of me? No, they would receive me as their father, just as Adam received his Father.

Brigham Young, April 20, 1856, *Journal of Discourses*, vol. 3, p. 319.

SELF-GOVERNMENT — MYSTERIES — RECREATION AND AMUSEMENTS, NOT IN THEMSELVES SINFUL — TITHING — ADAM, OUR FATHER AND OUR GOD.

A SERMON DELIVERED BY PRESIDENT BRIGHAM YOUNG, IN THE TABERNACLE, GREAT SALT LAKE CITY, APRIL 9, 1852.

It is my intention to preach several discourses this evening, but how many I do not know.

I will in the first place bear testimony to the truth of many remarks made by brother Hunter, and especially his exhortation to the Seventies and Elders, and those men who wish to go on missions. I wish also to urge the necessity of your proceeding on your missions immediately, and of going to the place of your destination full of the Holy Ghost, preaching righteousness to the people ; and while you do this, live up to the principles you preach, that you may teach also by your example, as well as by precept. Go, ye Elders, and now consider yourselves from this time forth missionaries. If the Gospel is in you like a flaming fire, to be poured upon the people, gather your neighbors together, and give your brethren an invitation to your house, and set before them the duties of man ; and preach, if you can speak but for five minutes, occupying that time to the best advantage. Continue to preach, study, and learn, by faith and prayer, until your minds and mouths are opened, and you understand most perfectly the love of Christ.

It is not uncommon for Elders to say, " If I could have a mission, and be sent among strangers, I could speak to them, because they have not been instructed in the way of life and salvation : I could lay before them the principles of the Gospel, which have been taught to me, without that diffidence of feeling, and fear, which I experience while speaking to my brethren." It is very true that the first principles of the Gospel taught by the Elders of this Church are easy to be understood, compared with what it is to preach them to our families, or to our neighborhood, and to govern and control ourselves by the principles of righteousness which the Gospel inculcates. Again, to gather the Saints, to preach the Gospel to the world, and convince them of the truth, are much easier tasks than to convince men that you can master yourself, and practise the moral principles inculcated by your religion. That is a small portion of the duty required of you in order to obtain crowns of glory, immortality, and eternal lives. I will here remark, that it is natural for the people to desire to know a great deal of the MYSTERIES ; this, however, is not universally the case, though it is so with a great many of the Elders of Israel. I do not suppose it will apply to those who compose this congregation ; your object in being here this evening is not to hear some great mystery of the Kingdom, which you never understood before. The greatest mystery a man ever learned, is to know how to control the human mind, and bring every faculty and power of the same in subjection to Jesus Christ ; this is the greatest

April 1852, *Journal of Discourses* 1:46. (Note the last phrase in the page heading: "Adam, our Father and our God.")

lead me." I was trying to think of the place where God is not, but it is impossible, unless you can find *empty* space; and *there* I believe He is not. If you can find such a place, it will become useful for a hiding place to those who wish to hide themselves from the presence of the Lord, in the great day of accounts. I will close this sermon, as I intend to preach another before I present the subject I more particularly wish to speak upon.

My next sermon will be to both Saint and sinner. One thing has remained a mystery in this kingdom up to this day. It is in regard to the character of the well-beloved Son of God, upon which subject the Elders of Israel have conflicting views. Our God and Father in heaven, is a being of tabernacle, or, in other words, He has a body, with parts the same as you and I have ; and is capable of showing forth His works to organized beings, as, for instance, in the world in which we live, it is the result of the knowledge and infinite wisdom that dwell in His organized body. His son Jesus Christ has become a personage of tabernacle, and has a body like his father. The Holy Ghost is the Spirit of the Lord, and issues forth from Himself, and may properly be called God's minister to execute His will in immensity ; being called to govern by His influence and power; but *He* is not a person of tabernacle as we are, and as our Father in Heaven and Jesus Christ are. The question has been, and is often, asked, who it was that begat the Son of the Virgin Mary. The infidel world have concluded that if what the Apostles wrote about his father and mother be true, and the present marriage discipline acknowledged by Christendom be correct, then Christians must believe that God is the father of an illegitimate son, in the person of Jesus Christ ! The infidel fraternity teach *that* to their disciples. I will tell you how it is. Our Father in Heaven begat all the spirits that ever were, or ever will be, upon this earth ; and they were born spirits in the eternal world. Then the Lord by His power and wisdom organized the mortal tabernacle of man. We were made first spiritual, and afterwards temporal.

Now hear it, O inhabitants of the earth, Jew and Gentile, Saint and sinner ! When our father Adam came into the garden of Eden, he came into it with a *celestial body*, and brought Eve, *one of his wives*, with him. He helped to make and organize this world. He is MICHAEL, *the Archangel*, the ANCIENT OF DAYS ! about whom holy men have written and spoken — HE *is our* FATHER *and our* GOD, *and the only God with whom* WE *have to do*. Every man upon the earth, professing Christians or non-professing, must hear it, and *will know it sooner or later.* They came here, organized the raw material, and arranged in their order the herbs of the field, the trees, the apple, the peach, the plum, the pear, and every other fruit that is desirable and good for man ; the seed was brought from another sphere, and planted in this earth. The thistle, the thorn, the brier, and the obnoxious weed did *not* appear until after the earth was cursed. When Adam and Eve had eaten of the forbidden fruit, their bodies became mortal from *its effects*, and therefore their offspring were mortal. When the Virgin Mary conceived the child Jesus, the Father had begotten him in his own likeness. He was *not* begotten by the Holy Ghost. And who is the Father ? He is the first of the human family ; and when he took a tabernacle, it was begotten by *his Father* in heaven, after the same manner as the tabernacles of Cain, Abel, and the rest of the sons and daughters of Adam and Eve ; from the fruits of the earth, the first earthly tabernacles were originated by the Father, and so on in succession. I could tell you much more about this ; but were I to tell you the whole truth, blasphemy would be nothing to it, in the estimation of the superstitious and over-righteous of mankind. However, I have told you the truth as far as I have gone. I have heard men preach upon the divinity of Christ, and exhaust all the wisdom they possessed. All Scripturalists, and approved theologians who were considered exemplary for piety and education, have undertaken to expound on this subject, in every age of the Christian era ; and after they have done all, they are obliged to conclude by exclaiming "great is the mystery of godliness." and tell nothing.

It is true that the earth was organized by three distinct characters, namely, Eloheim, Yahovah, and Michael, these three forming a quorum, as in all heavenly bodies, and in organizing element, perfectly represented in the Deity, as Father, Son, and Holy Ghost.

Again, they will try to tell how the divinity of Jesus is joined to his humanity, and exhaust all their mental faculties, and wind up with this profound language, as describing the soul of man, "it is an immaterial substance ! " What a learned idea ! Jesus, our elder brother, was begotten in the flesh by the same character that was in the garden of Eden, and who is our Father in Heaven. Now, let all who may hear these doctrines, pause before they make light of them, or treat them with indifference, for they will prove their salvation or damnation.

I have given you a few leading items upon this subject, but a great deal more remains to be told. Now, remember from this time forth, and for ever, that Jesus Christ was not begotten by the Holy Ghost. I will repeat a little anecdote. I was in conversation with a certain learned professor upon this subject, when I replied, to this idea—" if the Son was begotten by the Holy Ghost, it would be very dangerous to baptize and confirm females, and give the Holy Ghost to them, lest he should beget children, to be palmed upon the Elders by the people, bringing the Elders into great difficulties."

Treasure up these things in your hearts. In the Bible, you have read the things I have told you to-night ; but you have not known what you did read. I have told you no more than you are conversant with ; but what do the people in Christendom, with the Bible in their hands, know about this subject ? Comparatively nothing.

I will now again take up the subject of tithing. The brethren have done well. They have been willing and obedient, no people could have been more so ; for this I thank my Father in Heaven. I could not wish a people to work more kindly in the yoke of Jesus than this people do : the yoke grows more and more easy to them. It seems that every man will not only pay his tithing, but give all he has, if the Lord requires it : still I see wherein they may do better. I asked the people to day to assist to pay our Church liabilities. The offer of three or four yoke of oxen only, we do not want ; but I will lay before you what we wish you to do. By the manifesto which has been read, you have learned the precise situation of the property of the Church. What has incurred this debt ? Why does it exist in the shape in which it now appears ? And wherein could we have obviated the difficulty, and done better ? A fourth part of the money already paid out, did not come in upon tithing. This money we have had to borrow in order to keep the public works in progress. You may say, wherein could we have done better, for we have paid our tithing punctually ? But has that brother, who sent $100 back to the

DISCOURSE

By PRESIDENT BRIGHAM YOUNG, delivered in the New Tabernacle, Salt Lake City, Sunday Afternoon, June 8th, 1873.

REPORTED BY DAVID W. EVANS.

...place these things before the people if they would receive them! How much unbelief exists in the minds of the Latter-day Saints in regard to one particular doctrine which [God] revealed to them, and which [God] revealed to me—namely that Adam is our father and God—I do not know, I do not inquire, I care no-...

...came here, and then they brought his wife. "Well," says one, "Why was Adam called Adam?" He was the first man on the earth, and its framer and maker, he, with the help of his brethren, brought it into existence. Then he said, "I want my children who are in the spirit world to come and live here. I once dwelt upon an earth something like this, in a mortal state, I was faithful, I received my crown and exaltation. I have the privilege of extending my work, and to its increase there will be no end. I want my children that were born to me in the spirit world to come here and take tabernacles of flesh, that their spirits may have a house, a tabernacle or a dwelling place as mine has,"...

NOTE: Besides this transcript in the DESERET WEEKLY NEWS, June 18, 1873, the text of this sermon by Brigham Young also appears in the DESERET EVENING NEWS, June 14, 1873.

The Deseret News, June 18, 1873, p. 308.

JOURNAL OF DISCOURSES.

THE SAINTS SHOULD PREPARE FOR FUTURE EMERGENCIES — EVIL SPIRITS — THEIR POWER AND ORGANIZATION — THE CHAIN OF THE PRIESTHOOD — ANGELS ARE MINISTERING SPIRITS.

A Discourse by President Heber C. Kimball, in the Bowery, Great Salt Lake City, Utah Territory, June 29, 1856.

On account of the breeze that is playing beneath this shade, brother Brigham thought I had better put on my hat, but I never feel as though I wanted to wear my hat when he is present. I consider that the master should wear his hat, or hang it on the peg that God made for it, which is his head, of course.

I feel tolerably well as to health to-day, but I suffer much from bad colds, and have to be very careful, for I am often confined in my house with colds. I took a very violent cold here last Sabbath, by sitting in the draft, and I have not felt very well since, still I feel ambitious in the cause that I have espoused. The things concerning which brother Grant has this day been speaking are good, and I believe in his doctrines because they are true, especially in regard to our being one. I do know most definitively that unless we are one we are not Christ's; and I also know that if we are not one

with brother Brigham, our leader, we are not one with Christ. Yes, I know this, and my feelings are and have been with brother Brigham all the time.

I have learned by experience that there is but one God that pertains to this people, and He is the God that pertains to this earth—the first man. That first man sent his own Son to redeem the world, to redeem his brethren; his life was taken, his blood shed, that our sins might be remitted. That Son called twelve men and ordained them to be Apostles, and when he departed the keys of the kingdom were deposited with three of those twelve, viz.: Peter, James, and John. Peter held the keys pertaining to that Presidency, and he was the head.

How did these keys come to us? Did not Peter, James, and John, ordain Joseph Smith our Prophet? They did. And Joseph Smith called and ordained brother Brigham, brother

No. 1.]
[Vol. IV.

There are the " glory of the sun," and the "glory
"of the moon," and the "glory of the stars."

The children of Israel belong to the glory of the
sun. They kept their first estate. They are nobly
trying to keep their second estate on probation.
Let the devotion, the faith, the divine heroism of
the Mormon sisters, witness this.

> "Adam is our Father and God. He is the God
> " of the earth."
> So says Brigham Young.
> Adam is the great archangel of this creation. He
> is Michael. He is the Ancient of Days. He is the
> father of our elder brother, Jesus Christ—the
> father of him who shall also come as Messiah to
> reign. He is the father of the spirits as well as the
> tabernacles of the sons and daughters of man.
> Adam !

Michael is one of the grand mystical names in
the works of creations, redemptions, and resurrec-
tions. Jehovah is the second and the higher name.
Eloheim—signifying the Gods—is the first name of
the celestial trinity.

Michael was a celestial, resurrected being, of
another world.

" In the beginning " the Gods created the heavens
and the earths.

In their councils they said, let us make man in
our own image. So, in the likeness of the Fathers,
and the Mothers—the Gods—created they man—
male and female.

When this earth was prepared for mankind,
Michael, as Adam, came down. He brought with
him one of his wives, and he called her name Eve.

Edward Tullidge, *The Women of Mormondom*, 1877, p. 179.

14

Providing an Alternative

Have you ever tried to take a broken or dangerous toy away from a little child? What a struggle it was, until it finally occurred to you to offer something else more appealing. Then the child happily dropped the object that had been held in a grip of iron only seconds before.

The same principle applies to an adult's interest or dearly held belief in Mormonism. On many occasions, after we have presented evidence disproving the claims of the LDS Church, we have seen Mormons defiantly cling to the sect anyway with the challenge, "Can you offer something better?" Asking the person simply to let it go, without providing an alternative, is like asking the child to release the toy and sit there empty-handed. For the one holding onto the treasured possession, it is an invitation to embrace emptiness. It is unthinkable. But, when a more attractive substitute—genuine Christianity—arrives on the scene, the former treasure may become trash and may then be easily discarded without regrets.

Mormons confronted with the facts about their Church often express their horror with the rhetorical question, "If Mormonism isn't true, then what is?" They mean that there must not be *any* true church. They throw up their hands in an expression of hopeless confusion, almost desperation. This is because their situation is infinitely more complex than that of the child clinging to a harmful toy. For the child the toy is a momentary center of attention. But for the Mormon his religious organization can be everything. It holds within itself not only his relationship with God and his hope for the future but also the things he needs for day-to-day survival: a worldview that brings order out of chaos, a circle of friends who accept him as part of their "in" group, and a weekly schedule of activities that fills what might otherwise be empty hours. Mormonism is more than a religion; it is a way of life. How can you ask someone to abandon all this without assuring him of a more real relationship with God, a more dependable hope for the future, a more reasonable worldview, a more loving circle of friends, and a more interesting schedule of activities?

People who leave the Mormon Church without finding an acceptable alternative typically go into spiritual and emotional shock. Like the Israelites in the desert, they may wander in the "wilderness" for years, in a spiritual vacuum feeling condemned by God and without hope in the world. The largest percentage end up having no religion. Their gut feeling is that if Mormonism is not true, then nothing else is. In this condition they are prime candidates for return to Mormonism or recruitment by another cult. But most remain nonreligious.

So, not only is it difficult to draw someone out of Mormonism without offering a sound religious alternative, but it is also dangerous. Like thrusting a victim of hypothermia into a hot tub or suddenly depriving an addict of his drug, much harm can come to the person abruptly yanked out of a cult.

But providing a sound religious alternative involves much more than simply saying, "Come to church with me! You'll like it better than Mormon chapel services." It may be necessary to identify *how* your loved one became a Mormon in the first place, and then to reverse that process.

For example, many people are *reasoned* into Mormonism. They may have been perfectly content the way they were, but then comes a knock at the door. Two missionary elders ask a few questions about family values and religion, start a series of study lessons with them, adeptly augment the Bible with the Book of Mormon and other LDS sacred scripture, and spend an hour or two each week reasoning point by point with them on subjects such as modern-day prophets; priesthood authority; abstinence from alcohol, coffee, tea, and tobacco; degrees of glory; premortal life; sealing marriage for eternity; redeeming the dead; and so on. By the time the indoctrination program has been concluded, many aspects of life have been covered, and the convert's thinking has been restructured to the LDS view.

This lengthy process may have to be reversed when a person leaves the sect. Otherwise, as the saying goes, "You get the boy off the farm, but you don't get the farm out of the boy." The former Mormon may retain many of the automatic thought patterns that had been programed into his brain. Although not attending sacrament services he may still think, feel, and act like a Mormon. Even if he stops the use of the Word of Wisdom, that is, begins drinking coffee, tea, or alcoholic beverages, he may feel guilty or uneasy about it.

The best remedy for this is personal contact with former Mormons who have become Christians. They have already gone through the process of untwisting the twisted reasonings they had been taught, but they still remember how they used to think, so they are in the best position to help a member or new ex-member. Christians who *thoroughly* understand Mormonism can also accomplish this. It may not be possible to put your loved one in touch with ex-Mormons or Christian experts on Mormonism, perhaps because he or she is not yet ready to deal with "apostates," or perhaps because of geographical isolation. In this case you can train yourself to provide the necessary help by familiarizing yourself with the testimonies of former Mormons. These and books on the subject, will enable you to overcome many of the twisted reasonings and aid your relative or friend to cross the gap from cultic error to true Christianity.

On the other hand, some people were not reasoned into Mormonism, and so reason alone will not be sufficient to get them out. These are individuals who were originally drawn to the LDS Church because it filled an emotional need. That emotional need must now be identified and dealt with to help that person leave Mormonism.

You can be fairly certain that someone became a Mormon to satisfy an emotional need if any of the following are true: (1) He or she joined shortly after experiencing a divorce, a betrothal breakup, the death of a close family member, or other similar loss. (2) The person had just moved from another city or town and had not yet made new friends when the missionaries called. (3) The individual became fully involved in LDS activities immediately after the missionaries made their initial call, rather than after a lengthy study course. (4) There was a romantic attachment to a Mormon boyfriend or girlfriend, or perhaps even a one-sided romantic interest in one of the missionaries, at the time of conversion.

Door-to-door religions tend to catch lonely people because their missionaries make house calls and find them at home. Newcomers to a Mormon chapel are given a warm welcome, receive lots of attention, are invited back, and are asked to share in other gatherings and activities. The missionaries remain closely involved, serving as personal teachers, guides, or friends, assisted by a nearby member until the investigator is baptized. Then the local ward members take over. Such attention given to a lonely person is difficult to resist. It has often been called love bombing. A person can easily do whatever mental gymnastics are needed to accept or at least go along with the teachings of a group in which people starved for love and acceptance find those needs fulfilled.

A factor unique to men can be an emotional decision based, in part, on the Church's power structure. A man visiting a Mormon chapel may observe the authority and prestige of the leaders, desire it for himself, and discover that it is within his reach if only he will conform to the sect's requirements. This motive may not be overt or clear-cut; in fact, the man may not admit it, even to himself. But it may be a significant factor in his becoming a Mormon. Similarly, a strong desire to join or remain with the sect sometimes occurs when a man is dominated by his wife; the male-dominated organization opens to him an area where he can step out from under her control, much as in a men's club or lodge.

Whatever the emotional need may be—whether for acceptance, companionship, romantic love, prestige, or any other need—if the fulfillment of that need is a significant force holding an individual in the LDS Church, this fact is an important piece of information for anyone attempting to effect that person's liberation from the sect. Arguing doctrine or theology, even with the most persuasive logic, will produce no results, if it is neither logic nor reason that is truly motivating the Mormon. Like a lovestruck teenage girl who hangs on her boyfriend's every word, the Mormon who has found such emotional fulfillment in the LDS Church is happy to applaud whatever its leaders say. If you find your loved one reacting in this way, review the above-mentioned telltale signs to determine what emotional need is involved, and then consider how this need could be met outside the sect, perhaps with the aid of committed Christian friends.

In some cases the spell can be broken only when the honeymoon is over. After a while—perhaps a year or two after baptism—the new Mormon will come to be viewed as an ordinary member of the congregation. The courtship consisting of special treatment given to converts will end. No longer will the other Mormons go out of their way to be especially friendly, kind, and loving. The new member may feel like a newlywed who wakes up one morning to the realization that her husband no longer opens doors, brings flowers, or spends time holding her hand, but, in fact, has become harsh and abusive. Or the man who has attained a certain level of prestige may find that further advancement is unlikely and that the position he has attained has lost the fascination that it held when he was reaching out for it as a goal.

If such disillusionment occurs abruptly, this in itself may be enough to shock the individual into rethinking his or her religious connections. Usually, however, outside ties have been broken or minimized before this, so the unhappy Mormon has nowhere else to go and no one to turn to. Like the sobered newlywed who resigns herself to the drudgery of keeping house for an unloving husband, the Mormon feels compelled to keep up attendance at services and other activities for the religious master.

But this need not be the case. The Mormon is not legally married to the LDS Church. And there can indeed be somewhere else for him to go and someone to turn to if you have lovingly stuck by your Mormon husband, wife, friend, or relative until now.

The earlier discussions may not have worked, the proofs you presented may have been ignored, and the evidence you produced may have been discounted. The Mormon may have closed a blind eye and a deaf ear to every appeal to reason that you had to offer, because the sect's drawing power was emotional rather than reasonable. But now the emotional tables have turned. The member begins to realize that the LDS Church is not meeting his needs, while by way of contrast you have remained a loyal and faithful friend through it all. The emotional block to the anti-Mormon material you presented earlier may now be removed, and some of that evidence may be reconsidered.

If it is your wife who is in the sect, she will begin to see things in a different perspective: You "lost" arguments, but did not lose your temper; you respected her beliefs, although she did not respect yours; you put up with her spending all that time at chapel services and related activities; while she dutifully repeated what her church was saying about love, you were actually demonstrating God's love in the way you treated her. This can carry more weight than volumes of theological arguments or historical discussions. The disillusioned Mormon knows that she can turn to you.

Similarly, when it is a relative or friend who is involved, this assurance of finding love and acceptance somewhere outside the Mormon community is an important factor in the decision to leave.

Besides reasoning a person out of false teachings and offering a different source for the fulfillment of emotional needs, it is also vital to provide a spiritual alternative. The average person who embraced Mormonism did so, at least in part, because he or she had been reaching out for God. In the Beatitudes Jesus referred to such people as "the poor in spirit," or "those who feel their spiritual need," or "those who know their need of God" (Matt. 5:3, King James Version, Goodspeed, New English Bible). But, before the person could come into a fulfilling relationship with God through Jesus Christ, someone came along and directed him or her to the LDS Church instead.

So the new Mormon came to see himself in a relationship with God that depended on the LDS Church. God was at the top of the corporate structure, and the individual was at the bottom. In between were the local and general "authorities" of the Church, from ward bishop to apostles and prophets, a hierarchy too vast to number. The Church held the key to his eternal happiness, controlled temple rites, and provided the means for his eventual exaltation in heaven.

This was, however, a counterfeit way of salvation, a branch of the broad road that leads to destruction, not to God (Matt. 7:13–14). Jesus Christ is the one who properly said, "I am the way, the truth, and the life: no man cometh unto the Father, but by me" (John 14:6). So, the way to fill a Mormon's spiritual need is to point him to Jesus Christ.

How can this be accomplished? Unfortunately, some well-meaning Christians try to do it by arguing theology and the doctrine of the Trinity. But imparting these scriptural truths actually falls more under the category of reasoning with the Mormon to fulfill his rational needs and to correct his doctrines. *His spiritual need for a relationship with God is a different matter and should be considered separately.*

For example, there are clergymen and theologians who can explain Christ's deity and trinitarian doctrine with great precision but who are spiritually empty because they lack a personal relationship with the Lord. Many who were once in that condition have surprised laymen with their testimonies after coming to Christ. Therefore, we want to avoid the mistake of teaching theology *instead* of leading the ex-Mormon to Christ.

Once your friend has identified Mormonism as false and has therefore become teachable, begin to show how the LDS Church has usurped the place of the Messiah in his role as Lord, Savior, and mediator. Persuade your loved one to put aside the Mormon scriptures and books and start reading the New Testament, especially the Gospels containing the words of Christ, perhaps starting with John's Gospel. Encourage him to look to Jesus for direction, instruction, grace, and salvation. Show from the Bible that Christians can talk to Jesus, confident of his grace and loving concern for them (John 14:12–14; Acts 7:59–60; 1 Cor. 1:2; 2 Cor. 12:7–9; Gal. 2:16–21; Eph. 2:8–9). In this area your own example may carry more weight than anything you could possibly say.

The important thing is to help your loved one decide to follow Jesus Christ instead of continuing to follow a man-made hierarchy. Correcting his or her theology is a separate issue. Remember that the twelve apostles were all Jewish when they began to follow Jesus. They started out holding various opinions as to who he was, but they all learned as they observed and interacted with him. It took doubting Thomas months, perhaps a couple of years, as a follower of Jesus before he could finally confess the resurrected Christ as "My Lord and my God" (John 20:28). Since it may take your Mormon loved one as long as it took Thomas, ask God's help for you to be as patient with your loved one as he is.

Yes, patience is needed, because it takes time for people to rethink their entire religious outlook. But time may be on your side. Many who join the Mormons drop out again after a few years. Some formally resign from the sect. Others simply stop attending services and drift away. Commentator Anson Shupe states that two out of every five converts in Utah during the early 1980s eventually left, and that the First Presidency in Salt Lake City formed a committee in 1988 to deal with such "membership slippage."[1] Thus there is some reason to hope that a loved one who joins the LDS Church will not be in it for a lifetime. But many who join never find a reason to leave. What will be the case with your loved one? A lot will depend upon your being there at the right time not only with the right things to say and with convincing evidence to back you up but also with a loving heart and a personal relationship with God. You will need to offer an alternative that will satisfy the individual's rational, emotional, and spiritual needs.

See chapter 17 and appendix 1 for further discussion of rehabilitation and a list of helpful resources.

---

1. *The Darker Side of Virtue: Corruption, Scandal and the Mormon Empire* (Buffalo: Prometheus Books, 1991), p. 42.

15

Can This Family Stay Together?

Of the men and women who have phoned, written, or visited us after their mates converted to Mormonism, some have stated that they are seeking a divorce, that they are now living apart, or that they fear a separation is imminent. Can a family be kept together when one member becomes a Mormon? Or, if the bond is that between a parent and a grown child, between close relatives, or simply between friends, does the fact that one party has joined the LDS Church automatically spell doom for the relationship? Our discussion in this chapter will focus primarily on the situation in the immediate family, but the suggestions offered can be beneficially applied to save other relationships as well.

Close communication and intimate sharing of thoughts and feelings enrich a marriage, drawing a couple together. But this rapport is difficult to achieve when the worldview of one mate is a world apart from that of the other. A religious split between husband and wife can be truly painful. The Bible speaks of a married couple as "one flesh" (Matt. 19:5–6). What closer relationship could there be than that? A husband is counseled to love his wife as his own body (Eph. 5:28). So, when mates start to go their separate ways religiously, it is like a person's left leg going in one direction while the right leg tries to go off in another direction—very uncomfortable.

Religiously mixed marriages are often successful where both parties are adherents of mainstream religious bodies. But the more widely divergent the beliefs are, and the more seriously each mate takes his or her religion, the more tension there will be in the relationship. Furthermore, there is the troubling thought of the mate having a different destiny in the afterlife; this is especially a problem for a Mormon who desires to go to the temple, where an integral part of the ceremony is the sealing of marriage for time and eternity—a ritual that can be performed only with another Mormon. Also at issue is the matter of religious training for the children: What they will be taught and with whom they will fellowship. Problems can be expected if the wife feels obligated to preach LDS doctrine to her husband, whether he wants to hear it or not. Likewise, he may harangue his wife with strident lectures about the sect's false teachings and harmful practices. In either case, if the listener responds in kind, the resulting argument tends to escalate in loudness and in bitterness. This, in turn, leads to such frustration on both sides that they stop speaking to each other on that subject, if they do not cease communication altogether. Added tension will be caused by the busy schedule of activities that the Mormon must engage in without the mate.

So, there is certainly plenty of potential for marriage problems. First, the motives of the parties involved need to be honestly examined. All too often the new religion is simply an excuse used by a mate who had already wanted, either consciously or subconsciously, to end the marriage and who has finally found a respectable reason for doing so. It may be that the one who has embraced Mormonism has done so knowing this will be the last straw that will convince the spouse to depart. Or the Mormon convert may sense that the LDS Church will support his or her desire to leave an unbelieving spouse. It may be the non-Mormon who feels that friends will understand his leaving a wife who has joined a cult, whereas they might not have sympathized if he had admitted to simply losing interest in the marriage.

The new religion sometimes becomes a scapegoat for the one who has wanted to get a divorce anyway, for other reasons. If this is the case, nothing that can be said or done about Mormonism will have any effect on the situation. The religious issue is just a smoke screen hiding the genuine problem. If you perceive that this describes your situation with your mate, the best thing to do would be to seek professional help—preferably a secular marriage counselor acceptable to both parties—and to work at resolving the real obstacles rather than to allow either party to excuse himself or herself and deceive others with the religious scapegoat.

Suppose that it really *is* the religious difference that is at issue and that imperils the marriage. It should be noted that Christians who believe in the Bible find no divine injunction to divorce a mate who joins a false religion. To the contrary, the Bible encourages the Christian to remain married: "If any brother hath a wife that believeth not, and she be pleased to dwell with him, let him not put her away. And the woman which hath a husband that believeth not, and if he be pleased to dwell with her, let her not leave him" (1 Cor. 7:12–13). Unfortunately, immature Christians sometimes see matters differently and may actually encourage separation from a Mormon mate. The pressure to divorce may come from the Mormon side. Local LDS Church leaders have been known to encourage members to leave a non-Mormon mate, especially an ex-Mormon mate.[1]

But if you are a Christian who realizes that God hates divorce (Mal. 2:16), there are ways that you can make your marriage work, even though your mate has become a Mormon and seems determined to remain one. Unless your spouse is absolutely determined to end the marriage, you can do a lot to keep the peace.

First, before looking at methods for obtaining cooperation from your spouse, you would do well to look at yourself and how you fit into the picture. If you see self-pity or belligerence in the mirror, it is important to work at eliminating it, since it can be as destructive to the marriage as anything your mate could do. Ask yourself if self-pity is truly justified. Don't marriage partners pledge faithfulness "for better or for worse, in sickness and in health"? Aren't there many who find themselves with a mate who

1. In the case of Mormon Sheila Garrigus, when it became clear that her husband, Jim, had made a final decision not to join the LDS Church, her Mormon bishop visited and gave her this counsel: "Jim has made a sincere decision, and now you, Sheila, need to make a decision. There are three choices open to you. The first choice is that you could divorce Jim, because you as a believer should not be yoked with a nonbeliever gentile. As much as I like Jim, this is a real choice for you. Your second choice is to remain married to Jim for a time, stay in the church and raise your children in the church. At the time of your death, you will become a ministering angel. Or, you can stay married, remain faithful to the church, and at the time of your death you can be vicariously sealed to a LDS man in the temple as his second or third wife" *(Why We Left Mormonism* by Latayne C. Scott, Baker Book House, 1990, p. 54).

has become worse in areas far more damaging to a relationship than a difference of religion? Moreover, isn't it true that there are two sides to most marital disputes?

The Proverbs tell us, "Where no wood is, there the fire goeth out" (Prov. 26:20). If you avoid adding fuel to the fire, arguments over religion may not flare up so often. If it becomes apparent that your mate does not want to listen to anything you have to say on religious subjects, you need not feel an obligation to keep pushing the issue. This would not constitute surrender or defeat on your part but would simply show that you accept the wisdom of the apostle Peter's counsel, where he wrote, "Likewise you wives, be submissive to your husbands, so that some, though they do not obey the word, may be won without a word by the behavior of their wives, when they see your reverent and chaste behavior" (1 Peter 3:1–2 RSV). Peter wrote that advice to Christian women who were married to non-Christians in ancient Pontus, Galatia, Cappadocia, Asia, and Bithynia. Their husbands may have been Jews hostile to Christianity, or they may have been pagan idolaters or worshipers of the Roman emperors. Peter recommended good behavior rather than argumentative discussions as the way to win them over. So, likewise, in your marriage to a Mormon; if he or she does not want to listen to your words on religion, preach "without a word" by your loving conduct and tender affection.

Sometimes it is said that marriage is a fifty-fifty proposition. But a person determined to carry out his or her marriage vows will find that there are times when it is necessary to give 100 percent, expecting nothing in return. The result is usually a better return than when one insists on giving no more than 50 percent and demands 50 percent in return.

Ultimately it will come down to the two of you. Do you both really want to stay together? Then likely you can make it work. Many others have done so. How? Basically, by applying the biblical principles outlined above for a good marriage—principles on which Christians and Mormons generally agree.

What if children are involved? For a Christian to see a child in the grip of Mormonism can be as painful as seeing the little one carried off by a kidnapper. If it is a neighbor's child whom your youngsters play with, the pain is real enough, but if it is your own children who are in the custody of an estranged mate bent on raising them in the sect, it may seem almost unendurable.

Every LDS chapel is full of children. Many have one parent who is not a Mormon, and virtually all of them have at least one grandparent, uncle, or aunt outside the sect (except, of course, in Utah, where Mormonism prevails among the population). The non-LDS relatives of such children suffer much distress over their spiritual state, and with good cause.

Unfortunately, neighbors and relatives outside the immediate family can have little say in the religious upbringing of children. Courts generally rule in favor of the parents, except when abuse or neglect results in parental loss of custody. As difficult as it may be, other adults must remain mere onlookers, at least as far as legal rights are concerned.[2] Naturally, there may be opportunities to make contact and to impart some religious information or assurances of affection, but these are not guaranteed. The only avenue that is always open is that of prayer to the heavenly Father of us all, remembering that Christ said, "Suffer little children, and forbid them not, to come unto me: for of such is the kingdom of heaven" (Matt. 19:14).

In a religiously mixed marriage the influence of parents on the children will depend on the two individuals involved. What actually occurs will be a product of the interaction of their personalities and will reflect each one's love, determination, wisdom, and reasonableness. No one can say that a certain course of events is inevitable.

As far as children are concerned, a family breakup can do lasting harm, perhaps as much as exposure to Mormonism while growing up. In cases of simple secular divorce, where there is no religious issue involved, it has been said that the children suffer long-term emotional damage, especially when they are pulled this way and that by estranged parents battling for their custody and their affections. Adding a religious issue to this only further complicates the situation from the child's point of view. Studies have shown that children tend to blame themselves for the parental

---

2. Grandparents' rights and many other legal aspects of custody and religious upbringing vary from state to state and change from year to year as new precedents are set by the courts. We are not attempting here to offer legal advice. To determine your own legal rights or obligations, a lawyer with expertise in the field should be consulted.

rift, and when religion is a factor, they must contend with the thought of offending God as well.

When speaking of the effect of divorce on children, some have said that it tears them apart. The Bible tells of a custody battle in which that was nearly the case quite literally. Two women who shared a home in King Solomon's day bore children a few days apart. When one infant accidentally died, both lay claim to the remaining child. After listening to their stories the king ordered his men to cut the living child in two and give half to each woman. On hearing this the real mother interrupted and asked the king to give her child to the other woman, so that at least it might live. But the mother of the dead child said, "Let it be neither mine nor thine, but divide it." Solomon immediately identified the real mother by her unselfish concern for the child's welfare and awarded custody to her (1 Kings 3:17–27). Besides demonstrating the wisdom of King Solomon, this account also points out that a loving parent might be willing to surrender a child to another rather than see the child torn in two. Similarly, in some cases a Christian parent has decided that it is better to let the children be exposed to the mate's Mormon beliefs than to tear the little ones apart through a divorce and custody battle.

Whether the family stays together or not, in either case it can be painful for the Christian to see his or her children exposed to LDS teachings. Yet, this is usually unavoidable. The real question becomes: How should the Christian mate react? Should the children be told that the Mormon parent is bad, that he or she is in a cult, that he or she is telling them lies about God? The Mormon may tell them such things about the non-Mormon parent. But, then again, he or she may not. And if such statements are made, what purpose would be served by responding in kind?

Ideally, for the sake of the children, the parents will be able to reach some sort of compromise. The children could go to religious services one week with the father and the next week with the mother, until old enough to choose for themselves. Perhaps the couple will decide, at least while the children are very young, to emphasize the points that they hold in common, rather than those where they diverge. Perhaps they can agree to disagree agreeably, letting the older children know that they hold differing opinions on some points but that they still love each other. In cases where parents have taken this approach, it has worked well.

Actually, it is not the lack of agreement between parents that disturbs children but rather the bitterness and hostility that all too often accompany it. Children are accustomed to lack of agreement and can live with it. They believe that ice cream is better for you, while their parents believe that spinach is. They believe that a messy room looks nice, while their parents believe toys should be put away. And they may even grasp that mother believes a vacation in the mountains is best, while father believes in the beach. Disagreement does not harm children, but disagreeable behavior does.

Suppose, though, that a Mormon father or mother tells the children that he or she is right, that the other parent is wrong, and even attempts to poison their minds against that parent? There is no easy answer. But responding with the same sort of attacks against the Mormon parent is not productive. In such circumstances the Christian should find some comfort in two facts: (1) Children are very perceptive and look at much more than just the words spoken to size up a situation, and (2) their long-range interests may dictate a different response from what seems immediately appropriate.

Besides what one parent *says* about the other, the children notice also how their mother *acts* and how their father *acts*. They can tell whether a parent loves them and their other parent, and, over a period of time, they will make their own value judgment on what each one says. Even though they may not verbalize it, the children will realize which parent is the peacemaker, which one is firm but loving, which one truly has their interests at heart. Hopefully, both will. But, if one does not, the children will eventually discover that.

So, it is not as though it were a life-or-death matter to safeguard children from exposure to Mormon teachings during their formative years. Such exposure actually seems to immunize some youngsters against the sect. On the other hand, some youngsters who have been kept from an LDS parent may develop an unhealthy curiosity about that one's religion, leading them to try it out when they become of age.[3]

---

3. My son at the age of twelve or thirteen chose not to attend the LDS Church (John Farkas).

Encouragingly, the apostle Paul includes in his counsel for a Christian to remain with an unbelieving mate who is willing to live with him or her these words at 1 Corinthians 7:14: "For the unbelieving husband is sanctified by the wife, and the unbelieving wife is sanctified by the husband: else were your children unclean; but now are they holy." This should be a cause for optimism on the part of those who strive to keep their family together.

16

Warning: The Life You Save
May Be Your Own

Setting out to rescue someone from a false religion is serious business. It should not be approached lightly. Not only can a poorly planned attempt leave the member more hopelessly entrenched, but it can also put the would-be rescuer at risk.

"Who, me?" some readers may think scoffingly to themselves. "Why, I would never become a Mormon!" And we are sure that they are sincere and fully convinced in that confidence. But, so was David Reed, when he spoke nearly identical words early in 1968 concerning Jehovah's Witnesses. Then, a few months later, he went on to study with the Witnesses, was baptized as a full-fledged member the following spring, and remained in the organization for thirteen years.

"For there shall arise false Christs, and false prophets," Jesus warned, "and shall shew great signs and wonders; insomuch that, if it were possible, they shall deceive the very elect" (Matt. 24:24). Overconfidence has no place in dealing with such powerful forces. Recognizing your own vulnerability will be a good first step toward safeguarding yourself.

The second step should be to enlist the aid of others, preferably someone knowledgeable and experienced. But, if such an expert is not available, at least get some friends to be prayer partners with you. Share your research with them. Let them know when you plan to meet with your Mormon friend and what you plan to discuss. Then immediately after the encounter, regardless of whether it turns out to be a success or a disappointment, see your friends again to discuss with them what happened. Keep them fully informed of your efforts. Should you start to fall for some deceptive cultic argument, they will be able to discuss it with you right away and give you a different perspective.

Recognizing that there is strength in numbers, be sure not to fall into a trap where the odds are stacked against you, such as a discussion with a Mormon friend or loved one who "just happens" to be accompanied by two missionaries, a bishop, or another more experienced Mormon. Although you may have been practicing swordplay in the backyard, that does not mean that you are ready to take on the Three Musketeers. Yet that is exactly the sort of match you would be up against in such an encounter. If you find yourself unexpectedly facing such overwhelming odds, simply excuse yourself, saying that you will be happy to meet with your Mormon friend alone on another occasion.

Be sure, too, that you yourself are strong enough for the challenge. This involves more than simply being fully prepared to speak on the LDS Church; the strength of your own faith must be capable of sustaining you under test. Besides knowing what is wrong with Mormon doctrine, you must also know what you believe and why. The tactic cultists are taught to use when under attack is a strong counterattack aimed at what they perceive to be your weakest spot.

Counterfeit money cannot stand up to a comparison with the real thing, but someone who spends all his time looking at phony bills and never sees real ones could be fooled by a good fake. Likewise with religion. If you are going to do battle with a false religion, it is vital that you spend time in worship and fellowship with real Christians. Also, draw close to God in prayer. Counterfeit Christianity is pale and flimsy in comparison with the real thing. If your faith is solidly founded on biblical knowledge, and you know God personally through a close, personal relationship with Jesus Christ, you will be able to march into this or any other battle fearing nothing.

17

Afterwork: Gradual Rehabilitation

With so much effort directed toward freeing your loved one from bondage, once that goal is reached, you may have a tendency to breathe a sigh of relief and to say, "Whew! I'm glad that's over and done with." But your work is not finished yet. The one you helped escape will also need help to return to a normal life.

Some people exit a cult as a tightly coiled spring breaks loose from a restraint. The spring bounces off the walls and finally falls to the floor vibrating all over. Likewise, the ex-cultist bounces from group to group and finally collapses a nervous wreck. Some set out on a search for another church organization to replace the one proved false. Others become bitter toward God, religion, and anything else that reminds them of the past. A few may even turn to alcohol or drugs to escape the complexities of the real world.

Many ex-Mormons appear to live a normal life but actually suffer from haunting memories, nagging doubts, unsettled questions, and suppressed fears. They may even feel that no one but another former LDS member would understand, so they keep these troubling thoughts to themselves, continuing to be disturbed by them.

Seldom does anyone exit a controlling sect without emotional wounds, spiritual scars, and a sense of disorientation. And the longer the person has spent in the group, the longer the healing and re-normalization process can be expected to take. This is especially true of Mormons. They were slowly taught to think LDS thought patterns as they grew up in or were brought into the Church, and once they are brought out they must slowly learn to think normally again.

"Time heals all wounds," someone may quote the popular saying. "Just give her time, and she'll be back to her old self again." There is some truth to that, of course. Mormon leaders themselves know that constant indoctrination is needed to maintain a strong hold on their followers. Missing meetings is frowned upon, and staying away from chapel for an extended "vacation" is discouraged, because the message constantly repeated at the meetings begins to fade from the brain as soon as the foot hits the street. That is why Mormons are expected to attend Sunday school and sacrament meeting on Sundays, followed by priesthood meeting for men and Relief Society meeting for women, in addition to which men are expected to participate in home teaching and women in visiting teaching. As the old adage says, "Repetition is the mother of retention," and the messages heard in these meetings and activities certainly are repetitive and combine the indoctrination with peer pressure aimed at strengthening each member in Mormonism.

After a person has quit the sect, each passing day provides fresh food for thought, pushing the old memories further back in the mind. Time away from the sect weakens its influence. But time alone is not a cure-all. Like knots in a rope, each tangled reasoning or troubled thought must be dealt with individually.

Some people leave the LDS Church informally by becoming "inactive," that is, no longer attending sacrament services or participating in other meetings or activities. Such a person may continue to think of himself as a Mormon until Church ties are formally broken. So, just as the step of baptism allowed the new member to declare, "Now I am a Mormon," it will be helpful to your loved one in the recovery process to formally sever his or her connection with the LDS Church. Then he will be able to say to himself and to others, "Now I am no longer a Mormon." Local LDS leaders may take the initiative to formalize the break by excommunicating a member who has publicly rejected Mormonism and joined another church. Or the one leaving the sect may submit to them a letter asking to have his or her name taken off the LDS Church membership rolls. This is desirable and should be encouraged but should not be made an issue.

Severing membership ends all formal obligations to the LDS Church, but even some who take this step may still think it wrong to drink tea, coffee, or alcohol, or may feel guilty doing "worldly" things on Sunday: a secular job, yard work, home repairs, or any nonchurch work.[1] Some worry constantly about questions relating to God, the afterlife, and the nature of true Christianity.

An observer who has never been immersed in a cult may be able to brush such matters aside, telling the ex-Mormon, "Oh! That's just a lot of silly nonsense. Come on! You don't have to believe that anymore; you're out of the LDS Church now. Just forget all that stuff!"

The former Mormon may manage to smile and respond, "Okay! You're right!" He or she may even go ahead and do the thing in question, such as drinking coffee. But the problem actually remains and, in fact, gets worse, because now it is suppressed and is compounded by a guilty conscience. Unless the twisted reasoning is patiently untwisted, point by point, real healing does not occur. It is like a splinter that is not removed but instead is treated with painkiller, disinfectant, and a bandage. It may seem to be cured, but the pain will recur until the splinter is actually extracted.

Thus there are former members who left the LDS Church years earlier but who are still troubled by problems common to those who are just now coming out. Why? Because the root of their problems has never yet been fully addressed; or, because the people who have tried to help them were not really qualified and did not get the job done.

The indoctrination formerly received on a continual basis, although now rejected, has still left behind a residue of peculiar ideas and thought patterns. As a result, ex-Mormons start off with different assumptions from ordinary folk. For example, a roomful of people may listen to a minister preach the gospel. Quite a few of those who hear the message may accept Jesus Christ as their Lord and Savior and "come forward" when invited. But the

1. It is not our intention to argue in favor of such practices. Romans 14:1–23 leaves such decisions up to the individual believer.

ex-Mormon in the audience remains unmoved, or even confused, because what he heard did not make sense to him. In his mind, Jesus has already given him "general salvation," because this particular aspect of LDS teaching has never been cleared up for him. The words the minister spoke were sufficient to convince others in the audience, because they shared certain common assumptions. But the ex-Mormon had something altogether different in his mind, and the minister's message failed to deal with it.

A few people manage to deprogram themselves upon leaving the LDS Church; such individuals are usually readers who spend a lot of time alone with the Bible and with other books that help them gain a new worldview. Some married couples deprogram each other by discussing what they used to believe and what to believe now, while each one receives fresh insight through reading and through contact with workmates or neighbors. They share these new thoughts, gradually stripping themselves of their former belief structure. But most ex-Mormons need some form of outside help to successfully shed the mental baggage they have been saddled with by their former mentors.

If you are engaged in helping someone in this position, then you should be prepared to assist this thought transformation. Transporting a person physically out of a Mormon chapel and into a Christian church is a major accomplishment. But the changes taking place inside the person are what really count, and those changes take place gradually over a long period of time. A lot of patient assistance is needed, both before and after the break with the sect.

You will be able to initiate some of the discussion required to help a former Mormon rethink his or her beliefs. But many other points will have to be addressed when they happen to come up in the individual's mind; you will need to make yourself available to be called upon at such times.

You can also provide supplementary assistance by putting the ex-member in touch with others who have gone through a similar experience. In some localities there are support groups for former cultists, some specifically for ex-Mormons.

But caution must be exercised in selecting such associations, since, in some cases, persons who are only half out of Mormonism get together to perpetuate their shared beliefs. A few individuals who are all just leaving the sect at the same time may find each other and get together for mutual support; they all need help, but there is no one among them competent to give help. The blind end up leading the blind. They share the same problem, but none of them has yet found the solution. The result is that the group stagnates, functioning as an entity separate from the LDS Church but retaining many of the strange notions that its members still have in common.

Therefore, before you put your friend in touch with a support group or ministry, or before you pass on a book or tape, you would do well to first assure yourself that the group, author, or speaker is truly free.

For those in areas distant from wholesome ex-Mormon association, there are newsletters and fellowships formed through the mail. And there are books of testimonies and admonition written by former members.

For assistance in finding valid ministries, support groups, and resources, see appendix 1.

Resources and Support Groups

Because the person battling Mormonism needs all the help he or she can get, we list here a number of publications, ministries, and local support groups that may be of assistance.

Mormon Sacred Scripture or *Standard Works*

The Holy Bible, Authorized King James Version with Explanatory Notes and Cross References to the Standard Works of the Church of Jesus Christ of Latter-day Saints. The Church of Jesus Christ of Latter-day Saints, Salt Lake City, 1990.

Book of Mormon. The Church of Jesus Christ of Latter-day Saints, Salt Lake City, 1990.

Doctrine and Covenants. The Church of Jesus Christ of Latter-day Saints, Salt Lake City, 1990.

Pearl of Great Price. The Church of Jesus Christ of Latter-day Saints, Salt Lake City, 1990.

(Note: Pearl of Great Price is commonly bound in one volume with Doctrine and Covenants; or the three unique scriptures of Mormonism—the Book of Mormon, Doctrine and Covenants, and Pearl of Great Price—may be bound together as a single volume.)

Other Pro-Mormon Publications

A Marvelous Work and a Wonder. LeGrand Richards (a Mormon Apostle). Salt Lake City: Deseret Book Company, 1976 and 1979 editions.

Achieving a Celestial Marriage. A teaching manual written and published by The Church of Jesus Christ of Latter-day Saints, Salt Lake City, 1976 edition.

Articles of Faith. James E. Talmage (a Mormon Apostle). The Church of Jesus Christ of Latter-day Saints, Salt Lake City, 1952 and 1987 editions. (Certain other editions are paged differently.)

Gospel Principles. A teaching manual written and published by The Church of Jesus Christ of Latter-day Saints, Salt Lake City, 1986 edition.

Jesus the Christ: A Study of the Messiah and His Mission according to Holy Scriptures both Ancient and Modern. James E. Talmage (a Mormon Apostle). Salt Lake City: Deseret Book Company, 1975 edition.

Mormon Doctrine. Bruce R. McConkie (a Mormon Apostle). Salt Lake City: Bookcraft, 2nd ed., 1979.

Mormon Experience, The. Leonard J. Arrington and Davis Bitton. New York: Vintage Books, 1980.

Teachings of the Prophet Joseph Smith. Compiled by Joseph Fielding Smith (a Mormon Apostle). Salt Lake City: Deseret Book Company, 1976.

Critical Works

Adam-God. Craig L. Thalson. Payson, Utah: Publishment, 1991.

Adam-God Maze, ·The. Culley Christensen, M.D. Scottsdale, Ariz.: Independent Publishers, 1981.

"And this is Life Eternal that they might know Thee, the only True God" ¿Adam? Melaine Layton. Self-published, no date. Melaine Layton, 4383 Ruskin Road, Rockford, IL 61101.

By His Own Hand Upon Papyrus. Charles M. Larson. Grand Rapids: Institute for Religious Research, 1985, revised 1992.

3,913 Changes in the Book of Mormon: A Photo Reprint of the Original 1830 Edition of The Book of Mormon With all the

Changes Marked. Jerald and Sandra Tanner. Salt Lake City: Utah Lighthouse Ministry, no date.

Changing World of Mormonism, The. Jerald and Sandra Tanner. Chicago: Moody Press, 1980.

God's Word, Final, Infallible and Forever. Floyd McElveen. Grand Rapids: Gospel Truths Ministries, 1985.

Kingdom of the Cults, The. Walter R. Martin. Minneapolis: Bethany House Publishers, 1977 edition.

Mormon Claims Answered. Marvin W. Cowan. Salt Lake City: self-published, 1984 and 1989 editions.

Mormon Illusion, The. Floyd C. McElveen. Ventura, Calif.: Regal Books, 1979 edition.

Mormon Polygamy—A History. Richard S. Van Wagoner. Salt Lake City: Signature Books, 1986.

Mormonism, Mama, and Me. Thelma "Granny" Geer. Chicago: Moody Press, 1986 edition.

Mormonism—Shadow or Reality? Jerald and Sandra Tanner. Salt Lake City: Utah Lighthouse Ministry, 1972 enlarged edition.

Mormons Answered Verse by Verse. David A. Reed and John R. Farkas. Grand Rapids: Baker Book House, 1992.

No Man Knows My History. Fawn M. Brodie. New York: Alfred A. Knopf, 2nd ed., 1971.

On the Frontlines Witnessing to Mormons. Wally Tope. La Cañada Flintridge, Calif.: Frontline Ministries, 1981 edition.

Unholy Devotion: Why Cults Lure Christians. Harold L. Busséll. Grand Rapids: Zondervan Publishing House, 1983.

Use of the Bible in the Book of Mormon, The. H. Michael Marquardt. St. Louis: Personal Freedom Outreach, 1979.

Where Does It Say That? Bob Witte. Grand Rapids: Gospel Truths Ministries, no date.

Why We Left Mormonism. Latayne C. Scott. Grand Rapids: Baker Book House, 1990.

Witnessing to the Mormons. Jerry and Marian Bodine. San Juan Capistrano, Calif.: Christian Research Institute, 1978.

Note: There are many other excellent books on Mormonism and cults in general. Those listed above are a few that we believe the average reader with a loved one in the sect will find most helpful. A number of other useful books, booklets, and newsletters have been self-published by the various ministries noted below.

Ministries and Support Groups

Alpha & Omega Ministries, P.O. Box 47041, Phoenix, AZ 85086. Newsletter, booklets, tracts, traveling speakers, 24-hour recorded message for LDS (602-266-2LDS).

Berean Christian Ministries, P.O. Box 1091, Webster, NY 14580. Newsletter, books, tapes, tracts, counseling, traveling speakers. (This is the ministry of John R. Farkas, an ex-Mormon and one of the authors of this book.)

Christian Research Institute, P.O. Box 500, San Juan Capistrano, CA 92693. Magazine, books, radio program, tracts.

Comments from the Friends, P.O. Box 840, Stoughton, MA 02072. Newsletter, books, tapes. (This is the ministry of David A. Reed, one of the authors of this book, ministering primarily to Jehovah's Witnesses.)

Ex-Mormons and Christian Alliance, P.O. Box 530, Orangevale, CA 95662. Films, tapes, books, leaflets, counseling, and special help for persons leaving Mormonism.

Intermountain Christian Ministries, P.O. Box 21322, Salt Lake City, UT 84121. Newsletter, multilingual traveling speaker.

MacGregor Ministries, P.O. Box 73, Balfour, B.C. V0G 1C0, Canada. Newsletter, books, tapes, tracts, traveling speakers.

Mormonism Research Ministry, P.O. Box 20705, El Cajon, CA 92021. Films, tapes, books, newsletter, lectures, radio program.

Personal Freedom Outreach, P.O. Box 26062, St Louis, MO 63136. Newsletter, books, tapes, videos, traveling speakers.

Utah Lighthouse Ministries, P.O. Box 1884, Salt Lake City, UT 84110. Films, tapes, books, newsletter, copies of rare documents.

Utah Missions, P.O. Box 348, Marlow, OK 73055. Films, tapes, books, leaflets, newspaper.

Watchman Fellowship, P.O. Box 13251, Arlington, TX 76094. Newsletter, books, tracts, tapes, videos, traveling speakers, 24-hour message for LDS (817-461-1900).

Note: Those listed above represent only a sampling of the many local ministries and support groups—primarily the largest, those staffed by former Mormons, and those most likely to be able to refer inquirers to sources of help closer to home. For a more complete list of such ministries and support groups, please see the *Directory of Cult Research Organizations*, published annually by Cornerstone Press, 4707 N. Malden St., Chicago, IL 60640.

The authors of *How to Rescue Your Loved One from Mormonism* have computerized listings of hundreds of contacts across the United States. If you wish to find help in your locality, or if you have questions or comments concerning this book, you may write John R. Farkas, Berean Christian Ministries, P.O. Box 1091, Webster, NY 14580.

Data Discussed in Chapter 9
"The Fruits of Mormonism"

	Year	Births/1000 population	Abortions/1000 live births	Deaths/1000 population	Violent crime/100,000 pop.	Property crime/100,000 pop.	Total crime/100,000 pop.	Rapes/100,000 pop.
U.S.	'80	15.9	428	8.8	597		5950	36.4
	'83	15.5	436	8.6	538		5175	33.7
	'84	15.5	422	8.6	539		5031	35.7
	'85	15.8	425	8.7	556		5237	36.6
	'86	15.6	416	8.7	617			37.5
	'87	15.7	406	8.7	610	4940	5550	37.4
	'88	15.9	404	8.8	637	5027	5664	38.0
	'89			8.8	663	5078	5741	38.0
Average		**15.7**	**420**	**8.7**	**595**	**5015**	**5478**	**36.7**
% high			265%	58%	144%			50%
Utah	'80	28.6	97	5.6			5881	27.4
	'83	24.4		5.3			5118	24.9
	'84	23.6	108	5.5			4766	20.3
	'85	22.8	116	5.5			5317	23.2
	'86	21.9		5.4				25.3
	'87	21.0		5.4	230	5389	5619	21.7
	'88	21.3	139	5.5	243	5336	5579	24.0
	'89			5.7	259	5423	5682	29.0
Average		**23.4**	**115**	**5.5**	**244**	**5383**	**5423**	**24.5**
% high		49%					7%	

Murders/100,000 pop.	Larceny, theft/100,000 pop.	Suicides—total/100,000 pop.	Divorce/1000 population	Suicides—children 5-14 years old/100,000 of that age	Homicides—children 0-4 years old/100,000 of that age	Homicides—children 5-14 years old/100,000 of that age	Child abuse & neglect reports/1000 children
10.2	3176	11.9	5.2	.408	3.21	1.19	
8.3	2869	12.1	4.9	.602	2.90	1.05	23.6
7.9	2791	11.6	5.0	.682	3.24	1.26	27.3
7.9	2901	12.3	5.0	.820	3.04	1.23	30.6
8.6	3010	12.8	4.9	.753	3.37	1.11	32.8
8.3	3081	12.7	4.8	.735	3.32	1.19	34.0
8.4	3135	12.4	4.8	.701	3.78	1.32	
8.7	3171	12.6	4.7				
8.5	**3016**	**12.3**	**4.9**	**.67**	**3.31**	**1.19**	**29.66**
174%						28%	8.1%
3.8	3932	13.2	5.3	0.0	3.16	1.10	
3.5	3610	13.1	5.3	.65	4.74	1.95	
2.8	3437		5.0	.31	1.94	.94	24.0
3.0	3870	13.1	5.3	.91	2.05	.30	27.5
3.2	4074	14.7	5.2	.58	3.72	.87	29.4
3.3	4229		5.3	1.99	4.35	.85	28.9
2.8	4239	13.6	4.6	1.69	4.52	.56	
2.6	4289		4.7	1.39	2.86	.83	
3.1	**3960**	**13.5**	**5.1**	**.94**	**3.42**	**.93**	**27.45**
	31%	10%	4%	31%	5%		

Appendix 3

Communication: Breaking the Word Barrier

Problems often result when the same word means different things to different groups of people. For example, an American visiting England asked directions to the *bathroom*. But, stepping inside and closing the door, he was disappointed to find no toilet there, since the British use the word *bathroom* for a room set aside for bathing. To find the toilet, the American should have asked for the *water closet*. Similarly, a judge in the United States was puzzled when a prison inmate appearing before him for a hearing flew into a violent rage after the judge referred to him as a *punk*. By this term the judge meant "a petty hoodlum," but a policeman explained to him later that to prison inmates a *punk* means one who regularly submits to sodomy.

To avoid similar problems when speaking with Mormons or with persons who have recently left the LDS Church it is necessary to watch out for word barriers. Otherwise you may find yourself talking at cross purposes with the one you are trying to help. While you are using a commonplace word with its standard dictionary definition, your Mormon friend may be attaching a totally different meaning to the same word. The result is that you fail to communicate your point or, worse yet, you leave your loved one with a thought totally foreign to what you had in mind.

For example, to most people a *gentile* is a non-Jew, but LDS members use the word to mean a non-Mormon. And they use the term *investigator* to denote a non-Mormon taking lessons from their missionaries. So, if you overhear one Mormon say to another, "The person you saw me with is an investigator," the words may cause you to picture in your mind's eye a police detective—not at all what was meant.

Similarly, if you visit local Sunday morning LDS worship services and ask the people you meet to introduce you to one of their *deacons*, you may be surprised to find yourself shaking hands with a twelve-year-old boy, since Mormons apply the title to an office usually filled by youngsters.

Now, if communication on such mundane matters can prove so misleading, just imagine how much confusion can result in discussions on deeper subjects. It is important to remember that Mormons enter such conversations with totally different preconceptions. You cannot simply toss around such words as *salvation, God,* and *heaven* when most Mormons use those words to name concepts quite different from what you are talking about. It may be necessary to keep asking questions to verify that your listener understands your words the way you define them, rather than with some contrary meaning.

Here are some words you should be familiar with, as Mormons define them:

Aaronic Priesthood—one of two categories of ministry in the LDS Church, assigned primarily to young men between the ages of twelve and eighteen, but also to new adult male members.

Adam-God doctrine—the teaching by Brigham Young that Adam of the Garden of Eden is our God the Father, the father of our spirits and of the spirit of Jesus Christ, and the literal father of Christ's body—a teaching unfamiliar to most Mormons today.

Angel—a former human resurrected with a body of flesh and bones but not exalted to be a God; *or* a spirit being who has not yet attained a body of flesh and bones; *or* the disembodied spirit of a deceased human awaiting resurrection.

Apostle—one of the twelve men holding the second-highest level of authority in the LDS Church, just under the First Presidency.

Baptism—an ordinance of immersion in water performed locally for new believers, bringing them into the Church; but, see also *baptism for the dead.*

Baptism for the dead—a sacred ordinance performed in Mormon temples using living Mormons to stand in place of dead persons who are believed thus to be posthumously given the opportunity to be brought into the Church; one of several ordinances for the dead performed in Mormon temples.

Bear one's testimony—to declare to others one's belief in Mormonism or various aspects of it.

Bishop—an unpaid Mormon Church official presiding over a ward or local congregation.

Born again—baptized into the Mormon Church.

Chapel—a local meeting place used by Mormons, comparable to a Christian church building.

Christ—Jesus, believed to be a God distinct from God the Heavenly Father who allegedly fathered him by union with Mary just as our parents procreated us.

Cross—not usually used on buildings or worn as a symbol by Mormons who give equal emphasis to Jesus' suffering in the Garden of Gethsemane.

Deacon—an office of the Aaronic Priesthood in the LDS Church open to boys twelve years of age and older.

Elder—an office of the Melchizedek Priesthood, including young men in their late teens doing missionary work and wearing a name tag identifying them as "Elder [last name]."

Elohim—God the Father, the literal father of the body of Jesus Christ and the father of his spirit and of all our spirits.

Eternal life—the kind of life God lives in exaltation, with the ability to procreate spirit children.

Eternal progression—a faithful individual's journey from premortal existence, through life as a human, death, resurrection, and progression to become a God, and continued advancement in the afterlife.

Exaltation—eternal life as a God in the celestial heaven, the highest level of the highest of three heavens.

First Presidency—the man serving as Prophet, Seer, Revelator, and President of the Mormon Church (the top office), together with counselors (usually two) selected by him.

Gentiles—depending on context, either the non-Israelite nations or non-Mormon people.

God—although in a general sense, any resurrected and exalted human, usually used in specific reference to God the Father, also to the Son and the Holy Ghost, these three being viewed as three Gods but spoken of as "one God" in the sense of being one in purpose. (Mormonism portrays God, man, devils, and angels as all sharing the same nature, in contrast to biblical Christianity which shows the nature of God to be totally different. See chapter 8, "Gods and Goddesses.")

Heaven—the destination of nearly everyone who dies, but divided into three levels: telestial for nonbelievers, terrestrial for religious non-Mormons and backslidden Mormons, and celestial for good LDS Church members only.

Hell—a place of torment from which most nonbelievers are resurrected into the telestial kingdom; only apostates who consciously reject Mormonism and work against it remain in hell forever.

Holy Ghost—distinct from Heavenly Father and Jesus Christ, a third God who has a spirit body in the form of a man but not flesh and bones.

Investigator—an interested non-Mormon taking lessons with Mormon missionaries.

Jack Mormon—slang expression for a non-practicing Mormon.

Jehovah—the preincarnate name of Jesus Christ.

LORD—Mormons interpret this word in the Bible to mean the preincarnate Jesus Christ.

Marriage—besides the generally accepted meaning, also the sealing of a man and woman for time and eternity in a special Mormon temple ceremony.

Melchizedek Priesthood—the higher of two categories of ministry in the LDS Church, assigned primarily to seasoned members over the age of eighteen, males only.

Mother in Heaven—the wife of God the Father, the mother of his spirit children.

Polygamy—marriage to more than one wife, practiced by prominent Mormon men primarily between the years 1835 and 1890, but now seen as an offense meriting excommunication (loss of membership).

Pre-existence—the Mormon teaching that the spirits of all people were procreated in a premortal life by God the Father and our

Mother in Heaven, that our spirits were born and raised to maturity before coming to earth to obtain a physical body, and that the spirit of Jesus Christ was the first one born to our Heavenly parents.

Priesthood—a category of ministry in the LDS Church open to all worthy males twelve years of age and older, empowering them to act in God's name. See *Aaronic Priesthood* and *Melchizedek Priesthood.*

Prophet—the man serving as President, Seer, and Revelator of the LDS Church, holding its highest office.

Sacrament—bread and water used in the Mormon version of communion to correspond with the bread and wine used by Christ at the Last Supper to represent his body and blood.

Saint—a member of the LDS Church.

Salvation—a word that Mormons qualify in one of three ways: unconditional or general salvation is simply resurrection from the dead, granted to all through Christ's atonement; conditional or individual salvation involves entering the celestial kingdom through works of Mormonism; full salvation means exaltation to become a God as a result of temple ceremonies.

Scripture—the four *standard works* of the Mormon Church: the Bible (King James Version), the Book of Mormon, Doctrine and Covenants, and Pearl of Great Price.

Seminary—weekday classes for high school age youths.

Son of God—besides Jesus Christ, all humans, since all are viewed as the literal spirit children of God who procreated our spirits in the pre-existence. Satan, the other demons, and the angels are also called sons of God because Mormonism teaches that God procreated their spirits in the same way.

Stake—a group of wards, similar to a Roman Catholic diocese.

Temple—one of about four dozen large religious buildings around the world in which special ceremonies are performed for the living and the dead; off limits to nonmembers and even to Mormons who lack a "temple recommend" from their leaders.

Trinity—contrary to the Christian concept of one God in three Persons, the Mormon teaching that three distinct Gods, Heavenly Father, Jesus Christ, and the Holy Ghost, are one only in unity of purpose. (See *God.*)

Virgin birth—a concept negated by the view that God (a resurrected physical man, according to Mormonism) literally fathered Jesus in the flesh in the same manner in which earthly men father their children.

Ward—a local Mormon congregation.

Word of Wisdom—the Mormon teaching requiring abstinence from tobacco, alcohol, and hot drinks (tea and coffee).

For words not listed here see the subject index. For doctrinal refutation, see *Mormons Answered Verse by Verse* (Baker Book House, 1992).

Subject Index

Scripture Index

Mormon Scripture Index